HAVING MEN FOR DINNER

HAVING MEN
for Dinner
Biblical Women's Deadly Banquets

NICOLE WILKINSON DURAN

The Pilgrim Press
Cleveland

This book is dedicated to the vital cooking of my
mothers: Helen, Dolly, Janice, Ruth, and Jimmy.
Afiyet olsun.

The Pilgrim Press
700 Prospect Avenue
Cleveland, Ohio, 44115
thepilgrimpress.com

Biblical quotations are from the New Revised Standard Version of the Bible, ©
copyright 1989 by the Division of Christian Education of the National Council of
the Churches of Christ in the U.S.A., and are used by permission.

Printed in the United States of America on acid-free paper

11   10   09   08   07   06   5   4   3   2   1

Library of Congress Cataloging-in-Publication Data

Duran, Nicole Wilkinson.
    Having men for dinner : biblical women's deadly banquets / Nicole
    Wilkinson Duran.
      p. cm.
    Includes bibliographical references and index.
    ISBN 0-8298-1710-7 (alk. paper)
      1. Women—Biblical teaching. 2. Men—Biblical teaching. 3. Man-woman
    relationships—Biblical teaching. 4. Dinners and dining—Biblical
    teaching. I. Title.
  BS680.W7D87 2006
  220.9'2082—dc22   2006000629

  ISBN-13: 978-0-8298-1710-2
  ISBN-10: 0-8298-1710-7

CONTENTS

Introduction / 7

1   Jael: *A Tale of Milk and Murder* / 17

2   Judith: *Keeping Kosher with a Vengeance* / 39

3   Esther: *Sleeping (and Drinking) with the Enemy* / 65

4   Herodias: *Banquet and Seduction in the
    Realm of Wrong* / 85

5   Abigail: *Murder, Shalom, and the Lack Thereof* / 105

Conclusion / 127

Works Cited / 135

Notes / 139

— INTRODUCTION —

FOOD, DRINK, SEX, AND DEATH

The Symbolism of Eating and Drinking

The quickest way to a man's heart? Through his chest.

ROSEANNE BARR

WOMEN IN THE BIBLICAL NARRATIVES rarely kill. When they do, however, they do it with fascinating frequency in the context of a meal. In the succeeding chapters, I will look at five biblical women who use the power of food and drink, the banquet with its implications of seduction, to kill men or to determine whom the dining men kill. I will ask how the symbolism of food and drink interacts with gender, sexuality, and murder in the tradition.

Long after I chose the title for this book, a special edition of *US News and World Report* focusing on "Women of the Bible" included an article entitled, "Dirty Rotten Men: Biblical Bad Boys You Wouldn't Want to Have Over for Dinner." Who wouldn't want to have them over for dinner? Presumably, women. The focus of my book is not on men behaving badly or posing a danger to women—although such behavior and danger comes up along the way–it is about women who face and overcome the men and dangers that come their way. They are able to do this by having dangerous men for dinner and becoming more dangerous themselves than the men they might have feared. Whether or not each of these women is admirable is a point greatly debated throughout the history of biblical interpretation. Many critics argue about several, if not all, of these women, that they are simply another side of the coin of patriarchal oppression: women who step out of traditional roles, or redefine them only as exceptions to the rule. To the extent that they are not traditional women, many argue that these women are intended as examples to frighten male readers with the terrifying, hidden, murderous powers of the female—the very reason that women must be kept under tight control. Women and girls who hear these stories might also be frightened—frightened of being the object of fear and distaste that these female characters so often are.

While it may be true that ancient authors did not intend for us to admire these women—or at least not to view them as role models—it is equally true that characters often exceed the intentions of their authors. With the exception of Herodias, who is seen as emblematic of a world of evil, we will see that the texts are somewhat ambivalent about whether we should fear or admire these women or both. But more importantly, whether or not the text of Judges 4 admires Jael, readers who see Sisera as a potential rapist, or as standing for all those who use rape as a weapon of war, will certainly admire Jael for her resourcefulness, her ingenuity, and simply for her success. To the scholar of ancient texts, these women may not be admirable, but they are attractive. These women are attractive because unlike many women in ancient texts and in contemporary novels and films, they are not passive, not helpless, and not victims. They have voices and actions of their own, and if for no other reason, they demand attention.

THE HEBREW BIBLE, THE CHRISTIAN SCRIPTURES, AND SOME THINGS IN BETWEEN

These narratives happen to represent several different pieces of the canon, so some explanation for the lay reader of their placement seems appropriate. The story of Herodias comes from the Christian scriptures or New Testament and was originally written in Greek. Jael, Esther, and Abigail are stories written in Hebrew that became accepted parts of the Tanakh or Hebrew Bible, the Jewish scripture commonly known within Christianity as the Old Testament. Yet Esther's story was translated into Greek very early and with some freedom; consequently, "Greek additions to Esther" are a separate entry in some Christian Bibles. At times, I will need to refer to how the Greek version deals with the Hebrew version's questions.

This Greek version of Esther was part of the Septuagint, the Greek version of the Jewish canon. Included in the Septuagint were a group of writings composed entirely in Greek and seen as a kind of secondary canon within Judaism—among these writings we find the book of Judith. When Christianity began to prefer a Latin translation of the Old and New Testaments, these secondary works—Jewish in nature, but written in Greek—were translated into Latin and accepted as part of the Christian canon, though some referred to them as a second canon or deuterocanonical. The Protestant reformers, in their effort to strip away tradition and interpretation from the scripture, rejected this group of texts and translated only the Hebrew and Aramaic texts as their Old Testament. The book of Judith and the additions to Esther, along with the Wisdom of Solomon, Ecclesiasticus,

Tobit, Susanna, and others, were termed "Apocrypha," meaning "hidden things."

With the growth of ecumenism in the late twentieth century, many Protestant Bibles have begun to include these texts, but in a separate section, while Catholic Bibles will disperse the Greek books where they are found in the Septuagint, with Judith, interestingly, immediately beside Esther.

THE SEQUENCE AND SUBSTANCE OF THIS MEAL

Beginning with Jael's womanly, tently murder of Sisera (Judges 4–5), I will move to the story of Judith's use of drink along with the promise of sex to accomplish her superheroic killing (Judith), and then to Esther (Esther 4–7) and Herodias (Mark 6:14–30). These latter two women have equally deadly aim but use food and more importantly drink not to kill, but to manipulate the drinking man to kill. Finally, as a kind of exception that makes the rule, I will look at similar motifs dealt with in very different ways in the story of Abigail (2 Samuel 25). In the beginning, it would seem that the stories of Jael and Judith advocate a more direct subversion of the female role as nurturer—the nurturing turns to murder. Actually, all along, the nurturing role was a disguise for the female warrior. On the other hand, the stories of Esther and Herodias propose a more complicated and less subverted use of the nurturing role—respectively, they become positive and negative examples of the manipulative power of women's sex; the power to instigate killing, but a power that cannot itself enter the man's world of murder and war.

Like other species, human beings derive life from death—food is where we see that transformation. Whether or not human beings must in fact kill to live, sacrificial culture appears to assume this as a universal truth, often seeing even vegetable harvest as a kind of murder. Sacrifice assumes that we kill, at least plant life, to eat; thus we kill to live. It is fitting then that food should be prominent in narratives about murder, particularly those about righteous murder. Our texts require some justification for killing; no doubt more so when the killer is a woman. A useful and ancient justification is that this person must die in order for others to live; again this is the logic of sacrifice.[1] When is killing a good thing? When its proceeds sustain the life of the community. Thus, food embodies murder's primary justification and appears to lend it natural support.

I will look at both food and wine in these stories, and while the logic of meat as murder that sustains life does not require much argument, wine as murder may. As a vegetable product, wine may seem immune to associations with death. But a very rudimentary word study shows that wine appears most often in the Hebrew Bible in references to sacrifice. Occasionally, it even takes on violent connotations and associations with blood. So Judah, according to the blessing in Genesis 49, will wash his garments in "the blood of grapes" (v. 11). Likewise, Isaiah 63 describes the Lord treading the wine press alone, as though squashing human life rather than grapes: "I trod them in my anger and trampled them in my wrath (v. 3); their juice spattered on my garments and stained all my robes." And Jeremiah warns of the "wine of wrath" (25:15). More often, both in the context of sacrifice and of gifts intended to pacify, wine is mentioned in lists that include oil and grain, as the product of human labor, and in its connections with agriculture as a marker of human culture. All of these connotations will prove relevant to the texts at hand.

Ironically for these stories, there is a sort of anthropological truism that the sharing of a meal constitutes a community. Those who eat together become one—physically, as their physical substance will be reconstituted by the one meal they share, and socially, through the shared experience of eating and drinking.[2] The extent to which and the manner in which meals in these stories are shared point to what bonds genuinely exist between the characters and what bonds are part of the ruse.

The contribution of this book resides in the grouping of these particular stories and these particular female characters together for analysis. To the best of my knowledge, these stories have not previously been seen as comparable (except amidst a larger set of all female biblical characters). Yet once they are together, these five women have a great deal to say to one another, beginning with several elements of common narrative experience. Each story, except that of Abigail's, features a foreign male ruler—the foreign general, the foreign king, or in the case of Herod, a king who is both Jewish (technically) and foreign (in practice). The role of ruler in Abigail's story is played by David, whose definitive reign looms large, albeit in the future tense. In each case, a husband is at least mentioned, and his presence or absence plays a key role in the story. There are sexual hints or relationships between each woman and the man in charge, and in each case, food and drink are key to the accomplishment of a murder.[3]

The common elements, then, are a woman, her husband, a ruler (who in two cases is the husband), food, drink, sex, and murder. What emerges from an examination of these elements is the issue of power crossing gender lines. In each case, the woman confronts society's power, which is vested and expressed in a single man. Through the use of her traditional areas of expertise—food, sex, and sometimes motherhood—she manages to wield that man's power, the power to kill.

In the cases of Jael and Judith, the usurpation of power is direct and accomplished by taking power and life from the man; these are women who kill. To that extent, they become momentary warriors, taking on in the act of killing some culturally masculine qualities. The other three stories are more cautious, the women more manipulative, and their plots more complex. Abigail's story is unique, her manipulations, either so innocent or so subtle that the desired death is accomplished with no explicit seduction or murder. But in the end, none of these latter three women kill. Rather, they wield the man's deadly power through their proximity to him and by traditionally feminine means. Esther, Abigail, and Herodias may be read as castrating, underhanded, and no friend to the opposite sex, but they are not even for one instant male.

Having begun by looking at the motifs of food and sex in these murders, I was struck by their presence also in a sort of reverse mode—that is, by the emphasis on fasting and chastity in some of the stories. In particular, the story of Judith turns on her chastity and fasting, but Esther also fasts before entering the king's court, provoked by Mordecai's fast and summoning all her servants and all the Jews to fast as well. Perhaps most interestingly, John the Baptist is known for his fasting and general asceticism, which forms a kind of contrasting, condemning background for Herod's drinking party. Akin to the deferral of food is the deferral of sexual congress. Only Judith is explicitly chaste—once her husband is dead and forever after. Among the others, only Abigail's story holds no real sense of seduction. At the other end of the spectrum, Esther and Herodias are explicitly not chaste. Esther finds herself—like Jael and even Abigail, in a sense—married to the enemy. But while Jael is herself not an Israelite and her husband is no one to speak of, Esther's husband is the king, making hers perhaps the only biblically sanctioned marriage of a Jewish woman to a Gentile man, a situation fraught with tensions that Jael's methods cannot resolve. Herodias is married—illegally—to a man who claims to be a Jewish king but acts like a foreign king, and like a foreign king cannot keep God's prophet safe. Abigail despises her first husband, who himself is implicated in sexual immorality by virtue of his name, and who dines like a king and has the wealth of one, but gives place ultimately to the future king who will be Abigail's second husband, whose sexual immorality is reserved for later chapters of his story.

INTERTEXTUALITY: HAD ABIGAIL HEARD OF JAEL?

One question that arises in the course of comparing these narratives is whether their intertexuality is accidental. To what extent are the later stories written in awareness of the earlier ones? Certainly Judith has been seen as notably intertextual, alluding to Jael and Esther both. And the story of John the Baptist's death also presupposes the book of Esther, along with, I would argue, similar court legends. But does the story of David's meeting and marrying Abigail allude to the story of Jael? Both are tales of Israel finding an unlikely ally in its enemy's wife, though Abigail asserts her allegiance with words and food, while Jael's provision of milk is a deception, and her allegiance is stated only in the act of killing.

We will see other similarities between the two women's characters upon examining both stories. In the end, we cannot know for sure whether the author of Abigail's story had in mind the story of Jael; there is insufficient evidence for us to even submit a real guess. But my sense is that, other than Judith's more direct allusions to other stories, the connections between these five stories result from the fundamental quality of the issues they all touch upon. Alice Bach—to my knowledge the only other author who sees these characters as comparable along these same lines—notes the elemental nature of the food-murder-sex connections that fuel these narratives:

> The one who supplies food can be transformed into the one who offers death through the food she supplies. The nurturing mother becomes a murderer; the food that she serves— poisonous, intoxicating, magical—operates at the center of the trope. An offer of a bowl of curds precedes the killing of Sisera; banquet wine acts as a narcotic upon Holofernes. Food then takes on an aura of warning when women violate the primary connection they have to food and nurturing. This paradox permeates all the biblical stories of women who are murderers.[4]

Yet in another sense, all of these stories can be seen as rippling out from the story of Jael, the most direct and brutal of the five. There are no apologies for Jael's co-optation of the man's power to kill, and a keen ambiguity surrounds her possible use of seduction to facilitate the murder. Since there are no apologies at all in it, Jael's story makes us nervous. Its vivid image of direct female power shocks and thrills—the sexual tinge to the killing and its almost double-gendered nature are titillating as well as profound.

All four of the other stories seem to deal with the same issues in more complicated ways: spelling out the use of sex to facilitate killing in one direction or the other, saving the heroine from accusations that she is a temptress (Judith, Abigail, Esther) and a murderer (particularly Abigail), or condemning her as both (Herodias and her daughter). Compared to the banquets, food offerings, and/or copious drinking of the other stories, Jael's proffered sustenance is elemental; her home is not a palace or a city peopled with servants and counselors, but a tent where she is both initially and finally alone. We will begin then, with this bare-bones story, in the tent of Jael.

— ONE —

JAEL

A Tale of Milk and Murder

(READ JUDGES 4, 5)

JAEL'S STORY IS GRAPHIC, stark, and brief, albeit repeated. A woman alone offers shelter to a desperate man, gives him milk and a blanket (or two), then murders him with the first sharp object that comes to hand. Interpreters since the Enlightenment, when they have not ignored the story, have been disturbed by the woman's brutality and deception, and have found themselves unable to affirm Jael's killing as enthusiastically as does Deborah in Judges 5.[1] Feminist biblical scholar Katherine Doob Sakenfeld admits to having avoided the story because its violence offended her and points out that Jael's action is "wrenchingly difficult for many readers." Like most of us, she says, "I did not learn these chapters in Sunday School."[2]

Scholarship debates the relationship between the prose version of Jael's story in Judges 4 and the poem celebrating and retelling it in Judges 5,[3] but one effect of the presence of both versions side by side is that the reader has twice the narrative time to consider the story's implications. As we know, oral tradition relies on repetition for this very reason: It allows the audience time to process what is being said.[4] Some biblical editor or writer appears to have felt that extra processing time was necessary for Jael's story, and no wonder.

Remarkable for its shock value, the story is the first and only canonical tale where we see a woman physically kill, with her own two hands, and the man she kills is himself a warrior, trained and experienced in violence. Certainly Judith's story (on the margins of most canons) depends upon Jael's simpler and in many ways more troubling foundation; one could read Judith's story as entirely a rewriting, updating, and even a correcting of Jael's.[5] I would argue that Judges 4–5 hangs in the air for all the other stories we will examine here, unforgettable in its detail and unsolvable in its mysteries. Beginning with the writers of the chapters themselves, biblical writers, like biblical readers, have been unable either to fix it or to leave it alone.

Many of the unanswered questions that the story provokes surround the character of Jael herself. Even the meaning of her name has been debated: Perhaps it means "Yah is God," in which case the reader has an immediate clue which side she is on.[6] However, it may also mean "wild goat," in which case her identity as untamed and unpredictable would perhaps be emphasized.[7] Then again, it may be not a sentence or a noun, but a masculine singular form of a verb, meaning something like "he helped," in which case, "one might conclude that the proper name of *ya'el,* marked as masculine, is symbolic of the nature of her actions."[8]

In the same way that her name seems open to various interpretations, Jael as a character remains unplaced, identified only as the wife of Heber the Kenite, who is said to have left his own people and made peace with Israel's oppressor, Jabin (4:17). Neither the story in Judges 4 nor the poem in Judges 5 explains Jael's own ethnicity—is she an Israelite? A Kenite like her husband? Nor do we hear anything about her relationship to her husband, whose alliance she (as we later discover) does not recognize or share.

And just where is Heber, anyway? His absence makes the

story possible, as does his existence. The ill-fated Sisera would likely have no encounter with the wife if the husband were at home, as he would have no encounter with the wife if her husband were not Sisera's ally. Heber's character asserts no presence, but consists only of his ethnicity and his alliance (which are at odds with one another). His only action before the action of the story itself, is to "pitch his tent" away from the rest of the Kenites, near Kedesh, where the battle is raging (v. 11). His function, then, is to place his wife and their shelter into the fray, and then to disappear.

By striking out in opposition to her husband's alliance, Jael seems to be leaving herself at least momentarily bereft of any allies or support. Heber himself is an outsider, having left his own people to make this peace with Jabin. In doing so, he cut off himself and his wife from their primary support and defense system. In her tent in Kadesh, Jael's only connection is her (absent) husband. Once she picks up the tools of her trade, even that nominal connection is cut.[9]

Jael's emphatic presence lacks exactly the attributes that constitute her husband—known ethnicity and loyalty. What this means is that we have no clear idea why she would want to strike out as she does. Readers have been perhaps more disturbed by this ambiguity than by anything else in the text. For killing may be war or murder, glory or shame, depending entirely on its motive, and a woman in particular needs a good motive.[10]

Danna Fewell and David Gunn suggest that when Deborah and Barak have already routed Sisera, Jael's position as wife of Sisera's ally endangers her, unless she can dramatically prove herself to be on Israel's side, which she very effectively does.[11] Sisera is, after all, on his way to Jael's tent when Jael runs out to greet him (v. 17). She may have no choice but to receive him; he is an armed warrior with a prior claim, and she is a woman. Perhaps in self-defense, she goes proactive, running out to receive him in order to orchestrate the encounter on her own terms. He wants her shelter, her tent; she gives it to him with a vengeance.

IS THERE A RAPE IN THIS TEXT?

Other critics insist that rape is the interpretive key to both versions of Jael's actions. The poem's speculative portrayal of Sisera's mother raises this issue. The waiting mother explains her son's delay to herself by imagining him gathering up the spoil, including most prominently "a womb or two for every man" (5:30). The mother's mistaken assumption is ironic in the classic sense, since the reader has heard (twice) that Sisera is dead, killed by the combined efforts of two "wombs": Deborah, whose military leadership sent him running off on foot, and Jael, whose supposed safe haven proved to be his grave. As we will see, the irony has been heightened by the prominence in the narrative of Jael's womblike tent, with its ultimately lethal powers. Certainly, as Fewell and Gunn argue, by giving Sisera's mother these lines, the poem makes a kind of self-defense argument for Jael's action. We hear after the fact, third hand, from the poet speculating on the imagination of Sisera's otherwise unknown mother, that Sisera intended to, or could be expected to, capture and presumably rape the Israelite women, the women of his enemy. That expectation seems realistic given the customs of war both ancient and modern. Rape, as we know, often becomes a statement, a confirmation, or simply an act of conquest—the rape may constitute the victory, or it may announce and embody it. So, Sakenfeld reports, Korean friends and colleagues, remembering the so-called "comfort women" pressed into sexual service of the Japanese during World War II, have an entirely different view of this text, understanding it as Jael's emphatic refusal to become the spoils of war.[12]

Victor Matthews and Donald Benjamin also insist that the story implies Sisera's intention to rape Jael. Sisera goes to Jael's tent and not to her husband's for this reason, they claim, to rape Heber's wife and thus assert control over Heber's household. The alliance between Heber and Hazor, Sisera's homeland and Israel's oppressor, has been broken, say Matthews and Benjamin, by Sisera's defeat: "Hazor can no longer protect and provide for the household of Heber. The household of Heber has no reason to support Hazor and its armies."[13] Yet in this case, why should Sisera turn to Heber's household at all? What can he gain from taking control of the household of someone not his ally? No, it seems clear that Sisera goes to Jael's tent on the assumption that Jael will willingly hide him—otherwise, the tent of any Israelite wife would do. He might still decide to rape her; given the context of battle, the possibility is in the air. But rape does not appear to be his mission in coming to her.

More importantly, the idea that Sisera intends to rape Jael is weakened—as no doubt Jael's case in court would be, were she to plead self defense—by the fact that she leaves her tent to find him and somewhat insistently bring him in. Whatever he intends, she shows no fear of him, but on the contrary assures him that he need not fear her. Matthews and Benjamin note that the hospitality code cannot properly apply in Jael's case, since women cannot act as hosts, and Sisera transgresses the rules for a guest by making requests and then demands on her.[14] Yet their reading of her invitation, "Turn aside, my lord, turn aside to me!" as asking Sisera to leave her alone, to turn from his intended course and not rape her, seems strained, at best.[15] Far less effort is required to read Jael's words for what they seem to be, an invitation, and one with disturbingly sexual connotations. It would make contemporary readers feel more sympathy for Jael, no doubt, if we could see Sisera as barging in with violence on his mind, but in the story he seems more tired and thirsty, a violent man caught at a vulnerable moment, and he is invited into his destination.[16]

OF MILK AND A MAN

Jael invites the enemy in, leaving her tent and her social place to bring him in, as though hospitably. She offers him shelter, both literally and in the sense of security, shelter from the storm. Judges 4 uses the word "tent" five times, although the word is only used a total of twelve times in Judges as a whole, and the same story, told in poetic form in Judges 5, requires the word only once. From the moment we meet Jael, her tent as boundary and space, with its female shape and function, and with its implications of safety, hospitality, intimacy, and secrecy, is key to her significance.

Jael's first act in the narrative is to leave the tent, something she does twice, both times in order to invite a man in. In the Hebrew Bible, a woman leaving her tent puts herself in danger. Dinah in Genesis 34:1 and the women of Shiloh in Judges 21:21 leave their tents only to be raped. Jephthah's daughter goes out to meet her father just as Jael goes out to meet Sisera, but in the daughter's case, the going out will mean her death at Jephthah's hands. Thus, Jael's first action conveys an initial sense of her vulnerability. Whether this is meant as irony, given what follows, or as justification for it is unclear.

Jael's going out is an offbeat hospitality, it seems. She cannot be the host, according to custom, since she is not the (male) head of the household. Yet she offers some of what the host must offer—shelter, safety, and nourishment. Indeed, the succor of her tent overleaps its bounds, as she runs out to offer Sisera its shelter. He accepts that shelter at face value, having been headed toward her tent in any case (v. 17).

Sisera chooses this tent because of Heber's alliance with his people, and Jael's invitation seems to assure him that she honors her husband's allegiances. In Judges 5, Jael's hospitality to Sisera is celebrated as part of her clever plan to kill him. But the reader of Judges 4 might wonder exactly when she made this plan. Jael's motives are so unstated, so mysterious, that it seems possible that she welcomes Sisera genuinely and only later (on account of his behavior? as an afterthought?), impulsively, decides on murder. Further, as Elie Assis points out, the story of Rahab in Joshua 2 sets up Jael's offer of shelter nicely.[17] Rahab actually does shelter and hide men from their enemies. Jael's offer to do the same for Sisera seems then fairly plausible—we are the more shocked when the shelter turns to murder.

What Sisera wants from Jael seems to be quite basic—he wants her to help him survive. His request for water, among the most crucial and fundamental of all human needs, underlines his desire to live, and his fear that he may not. Aside from water, he needs shelter in order to survive—not so much a place to rest as a place to hide. So, the second thing he asks— or in this case, demands—of Jael is that she keep his presence hidden from anyone who might inquire (v. 20). For the biblical text, such a desire to live may appear cowardly and thus unmanly, coming from a warrior; later Saul will engineer his own death rather than return defeated from battle (1 Sam. 13:4). As others have noted, Sisera appears to raise the question of his own unmanliness when he instructs Jael, "If a man comes by and asks you, 'Is there a man here?' then you say, 'None.'"[18] He is, in a sense, renouncing his own (socially constructed) gender, refusing to be identified by men as a man, in hopes of saving his own life.

If he is not a man, is Sisera then in his retreat and desire for life, an infant? Although he requests water, Jael without explanation provides him with milk instead. This detail appears in both the narrative and poetic versions of the story, gaining significance through the repetition. On the one hand Jael's hospitality again seems to have gone beyond the expected, or even the requested. At the same time, in essentially ignoring Sisera's request and giving him something else entirely, Jael appears to take—or better, to maintain—control of the situation. In the whole short account, Jael never in fact does what Sisera asks her to. Water would in part have responded to the physical exertion of war, or at least of retreat; Sisera has been, we are told, running on his own two feet for some time (v. 15). Instead, Jael gives him a substance that sets her up as mother and nurturer, a drink that is nearly a food, and one with connotations of motherhood, putting Sisera in the position of her baby. If Jael cannot, according to the code of hospitality, provide what the male host would provide, she provides instead what only a female can provide, asserting herself both as provider and as woman.

At the same time as it invokes the maternal, the provision of milk also has sexual connotations, particularly in the intimate "opening" of the skin from which Jael pours (v. 19). As Fewell and Gunn note, the same word is used not only of opening a woman's womb in childbirth, but also of opening a woman's body to receive her lover.[19] The milk suggests bodily intimacy, which has both sexual and maternal possibilities. In the human world, those who might drink a mother's milk are not only her infants but also her lovers.

As though to emphasize that the milk is part of Jael's subterfuge, it is framed by two acts of covering. First, Jael covers Sisera when he enters the tent—apparently the man lies down the very instant he comes in, since in the next instant he is being covered (v. 18). And then again, when from under the covering he asks for water, "she opened a skin of milk, and gave him to drink, and covered him with a blanket." The Hebrew also allows the possibility that the covering is with a curtain, rather than a blanket. A curtain would separate the inner portions of the tent from the outer and so hide Sisera more deeply.[20] In either case, with Jael's every action Sisera seems to be buried deeper and deeper, disappearing—like a traditionally covered woman—until he is only a voice. Whether she ostensibly covers him to hide or comfort him is unclear; the point is moot once he is dead.

While he yet lives, though, Sisera seems to read the provision of milk and coverings as further assurance of his safety. It appears to be this sequence of covering and milk that signals Sisera to push Jael's protection further, telling (and not asking) her to stand guard for him at the tent's door. She and the tent—for she is the tent—will keep him safe, as safe as the fetus in the womb. He climbs into her womb, drinks her milk and, in the narrative, falls asleep, a fetus or infant, or lover.

In contrast to the other four stories we will discuss, the trouble with Jael's story is that the food-as-murder assumption does not seem to hold. That is, goat's milk avoids the killing connotations of other foods. Milk does not emerge from killing, but rather from the act of producing life; not from the male realms of hunt or slaughter, but from the female world of birth and nurture. What Jael provides to Sisera does not appear to have death as its price. Rather, it is the very essence of life—the spontaneous substance that all mammal mothers feed their newborn young, the thing that goats and people have most prominently in common. It is a tie to the "natural," the female, the world imagined without man's culture and its accompanying warfare, without the necessity of killing. A life-giving drink or even a food (curds) that does not necessitate killing, and thus offers no justification for the death it makes possible, the milk is in itself that much more deceptive. Those eating meat ought to remember killing; those drinking wine ought to know its violent origins and treacherous power, but those drinking milk? Those drinking milk are babies—sheltered from the deadly costs of human life.

SEXUAL, MATERNAL, LETHAL

Although in the poem Jael seems to strike Sisera down where he stands, in the narrative, Sisera's sleep is sound. Are we to attribute this only to the soporific effects of the milk, or is he sexually sedated? Moreover, we discover that he is asleep only after the tent peg has already gone through his skull—he's certainly asleep now! The sense that we have missed something also invites readers to assume that what we missed was sex. The scene itself invites a sexual interpretation; as Fewell and Gunn note, "at least in biblical literature, a man seldom enters a woman's tent for purposes other than sexual intercourse. The woman's tent is symbolic of the woman's body."[21]

Furthermore, Jael not only leaves her tent to approach Sisera, perhaps a culturally suspect move in itself, but phrases her invitation to him in terms that can be read as scandalous: "Come in, my lord, come in to me!" The verb *sur*, often translated "turn aside, turn away," or even "deviate, stray," together with its repeated sibilance, emphasize the secretive nature of Sisera's entry into the tent—he is turning aside, away from the beaten path where he will be sought, into this shelter.[22] In particular, the unusual and unnecessary addition of the phrase, "to me," raises the question in readers' minds whether the shelter and hiding place is Jael's tent or Jael herself, or whether the story in fact distinguishes the two.[23]

Sexual and maternal connotations seem to flow freely, often from the same image, in this story, and both are mixed with a goodly spice of death. Sisera's position described in the song, falling between Jael's legs, has connotations both of sex and of birth, but both are ironically invoked by a scene of death. In fact, the connotations of birth here must lead to connotations of aborted birth. Sisera believes this woman is mothering him, and he seems to become fetal in his trust of her even before she provides him with the milk he never asked for. But at that very same mother-infant/fetus moment, it suddenly becomes clear that Jael wants him dead. The poem portrays the conscious Sisera somehow struck with the tent peg while standing, at which point he falls dead between Jael's legs. As Mieke Bal notes, the killing in the poem resembles hand-to-hand combat and portrays Jael more unambiguously in the masculine role of warrior.[24] Sisera only arrives "between her legs" in death, though the place is most commonly associated with the production of life. In the poem, then, it is his death that looks briefly like sex; or as though Jael's womb has given birth to a corpse.[25]

THE TENT TURNS ON HIM

Most of Jael's short story in Judges 4 is taken up with her seeming hospitality and nurture. Until she picks up the tent peg, our only hint that she intends something other for Sisera than rest and nutrition is, ironically, her own reassurance to him, "Don't be afraid" (v. 18). When a warrior enters the tent of a woman alone, even if the warrior is in retreat and in fear for his life everywhere else, he has surely little to fear from the woman. On the contrary, the reader might expect Jael to be afraid, as a woman alone with a desperate man. As we have seen, the threat of rape here emerges in retrospect in Judges 5, when Sisera's mother waits for him to return with "a womb or two for every man" (5:30). Women are part of the victor's bounty; tragically, we know that women's bodies continue to constitute a battlefield in contemporary warfare. Jael's assurance to Sisera, then, seems to reverse their roles. Of course, Sisera *is* afraid of Barak, perhaps of Deborah. Jael is on one level simply assuring him temporary safety. Again, it is even possible that she genuinely intends to keep him safe at this point. But her insistent, "Don't be afraid," clashing as it does with expected roles of male warrior and female civilian, foreshadows what is to come.

Yet despite the warning to the reader in Jael's assurance to Sisera, she and her tent, her womb, appear as mother and lover to him, right up until the moment she drives the tent peg through his skull. Jael goes to him "softly," or "secretly." The word here translated "secretly" is used to describe the "secret arts" of court magicians in Exodus, and to mean something like "privately," as when Saul asks those near David to speak to him "secretly" (1 Sam. 18:22) or when Ehud tells Eglon he has a "secret" (and as it turns out, lethal) message for the king, which is then received in the privacy of the king's toilet (Judges 3:19). Ruth also goes "in secret," with the same prepositional phrase used here, to find Boaz on the threshing floor (Ruth 3:7). But Jael's secrecy is much less in her movement toward Sisera, tent peg in hand, than it is in the story up to this point. She has indeed gone to him quietly, secretly, as an ally and a mere woman, as a lover, as a nurturer, as a womb and a tent.[26] In the narrative, her secrecy, her softness, provides her with the opportunity she needs to do some not very secret or soft work. She goes to him softly to kill him with the tools of her tent—security, nourishment, mallet, and peg.

In the nomadic culture of ancient Palestine, putting up the tent was the woman's job, so these are woman's tools. The woman built for herself—repeatedly—the world that circumscribed her. Others admitted to the tent must be her children or her lovers. She raises the tent peg and mallet to nail Sisera's head to the ground, to the land, as the tent is nailed to the ground, for security, stability.

For this mysteriously motivated act, Jael is then, according to the song in Judges 5, "most blessed of women in tents"

(5:24); that is to say, as the parallel phrase makes clear, most blessed of women, period. For women are in tents, in the understanding of both versions of this story—the tents that are their homes, the tents that are their clothes, the tents that as clothes or homes are supposed to protect them from the eyes and aims of random men. Women are in tents and women are tents. Women's job in the biblical world is to be mothers, to shelter, nurture, hide, protect—to claim place for the organized processes of life against the demands of the chaos outside.[27] Jael brings Sisera into her world and nails him to the ground there—he will know what it is to be a tent. The verb used to describe the death blow is the same used to describe more mundane use of the tent peg—*taqa'*—it can mean simply to pitch (a tent). Her killing is thus paralleled with her husband's only action: "He pitched his tent near Kedesh." He pitched his tent, and in his absence she pitched hers in a quite different place. By murdering Sisera with the tent peg, she also makes the murder a part of her womanly efforts to construct the social world that is the tent. Sisera becomes part of the raw material with which she builds.

SUSPENSE, OR THE LACK THEREOF: JUDGES 4 AND 5

The shock of the (hypothetical) first-time reader at this abrupt turn of events may have something to say, incidentally, about the order in which Judges 4 and 5 appear. Although many scholars consider Judges 5 to be the earlier text, its celebration of Jael's act seems appropriate as an epilogue to the narrative. In part, the flow from the narrative to the poem is made possible by the narrative's dependence on suspense. As a character within the story, Jael depends heavily on Sisera's ignorance of her true loyalties. Within the story, she does everything (yes, perhaps even everything) to convince him that she is his handmaiden, his shelter and succor, and because she does convince him, she has the opportunity to kill him.

Likewise the story of Jael's actions depends upon the reader being uncertain, or even deceived, as to her loyalties until her loyalties become brutally plain. A first-time reader might initially see Jael as a reverse Rahab, sheltering Israel's enemy rather than Israel itself, and be almost as surprised as Sisera is when the tent peg strikes his head. Even the reader who knows what's coming winces at the abrupt shift in Jael's actions from nurturing to killing. Thus the reader is initially in the dark about who Jael is and what she is doing in the story, then learns what she did, and then, in the poem of Judges 5, hears her actions celebrated as a great victory for Israel. Unlike the story, the poem does not raise the question of Jael's motive or loyalties.[28] The poetic celebration, in contrast to the narrative, depends on the reader knowing ahead of time Jael's murderous intentions in order to appreciate fully the cleverness of her deception. The poem also works to clear Jael of any lingering doubts that she may have initially been in fact sympathetic to Sisera.

By celebrating her cleverness in having given him "curds in a lordly bowl," only to chop him down where he stood, the poem presents a Jael who suffered no ambivalence, whose nurturing actions were simply and only a ruse for her splendid warrior abilities. In effect, the poem muffles the doubts and questions of the narrative, telling the reader how to feel about what she has just read.

WHO'S THE MAN?

The milk, the sexual and maternal imagery of the murder, the emphatic tent, all appear to outline the killing with symbols of life. The penetration of the tent's phallic peg into Sisera's skull is thus terrifically shocking—who knew the tent had a penis of its own? If she had drowned him in milk, or smothered him with the mantle or with the tent itself, that would have seemed a method suited to the woman we thought Jael was. But in the actual act of killing, all the symbolism of female nurture turns out to have housed and hidden its own version of masculinity. Maybe this is not so much the dropping of a disguise to reveal the real, male nature of the power beneath, as though Jael were a kind of cross-dresser and this an ancient version of *The Crying Game*. Perhaps this is rather the completion of the revelation of what tents/wombs/women can do. Nurture, feed, shelter, conceal, and kill. But is it the mark of a male author's hand on the story that represents the woman's weapon as at once emerging from her own world, her own symbolic body, and at the same time phallic?

Jael's chosen method of killing has fascinated readers and become her most famous association. The way in which she kills him seems to say a great deal—though just what it says is under debate. One commentator understates the case to say that in the description of her piercing his head with a tent peg, "a certain amount of force is implied."[29] Mieke Bal insists that "the violence of the murder suggests extreme anger," and laments that "no one addresses this issue."[30] I suggest that if the story featured a man as murderer, we might be less inclined to see "extreme anger," even in brutality. This is war, is it not? But that is, in part, the issue. Is Jael angry, offended, frightened? Does she see Sisera as a rapist or has she simply been told what to do by one too many men? Or does she see him as an enemy, of herself, of Israel, or of God? Does she want, as Bal suggests, to join the fighting, even if she cannot leave her tent?

The story seems to say that women have reserves of shocking power and courage. Yet for the story itself, those qualities are only recognizable to the extent that their expression mimics the male warrior. Certainly, as male warriors were understood to do, Jael feminizes Sisera in the killing. Just as Sisera came "into her, into the tent," Jael now goes "into him softly," tent peg in hand. The brutal and emphatic penetration of the tent peg into "the thinness" in Sisera's sleeping head thus constitutes a kind of reverse rape. Fewell and Gunn, citing the Septuagint and the Song of Songs, read the Hebrew *raqqa* here as "mouth," rather than "temple," so that the tent peg's entry becomes yet more obscene.[31] The warrior turns out to be penetrable; the woman/womb turns penetrator.

There is, in fact, a great deal of gender-blurring in this story. Jael takes on the masculine role of host even in her provision of mother's milk, and the more primary man's role of penetrating warrior emerges from deep within her womblike tent. In the same speech in which Sisera, from fear, effectively renounces his manhood, he speaks to her with a grammatically masculine command—the verb *'amod,* "Stand."[32] The reader is perhaps meant to see the exhausted Sisera slipping into the language he uses to command his (dead) foot soldiers. Even so, Sisera thus treats Jael as a man and presents her to the reader as such, just before he tells her to say there is no man in the tent. Her response to Sisera's command and its ironic implication that he is no longer male is to promptly pick up the phallus he seems to have dropped.

> And he said to her, "Stand at the opening of the tent, and if anyone comes by and asks you, 'Is there a man here?' then you say, 'None.'" But Jael wife of Heber picked up the tent peg and took the hammer in her hand and she went into him secretly and drove the peg through his temple and it stuck in the earth....

If, Jael's penetrating action seems to say, you are no longer going to be a man before other men, perhaps you really ought to be a woman. The tent peg is designed to, and does, enter the grammatically and conceptually feminine earth, *ha eretz,* and receiving the peg, Sisera has become part of that feminine entity, a place on which to pitch one's tent.

After this momentary act of masculine war, Jael reverts to type, in a sense, again running out of her tent to invite a passing warrior. Jael's encounter with Barak is described in the same words as her previous encounter with Sisera—"she went out to meet Sisera," (v. 18) "she went out to meet him [Barak]" (v. 22). The two men are parallel, it seems—perhaps in their ignorance of what awaits them in her tent. The reader, on the other hand, having seen all, understands that to which Barak is invited. When Sisera went in to Jael, her motives were obscure to him and to the reader, but at this point much of the mystery has evaporated for the reader, and only Barak remains for the moment in the dark. David Gunn quotes John Kitto, in a mid–nineteenth century popularization of biblical stories, remarking that Barak, upon entering the tent and seeing the dead Sisera, "might then have pondered whether, had Sisera been the victor and himself the fugitive, the same fate might not have been his own."[33] Surely there is something unsettling for Barak in this paralleling of him with his vanquished enemy, as there is of course something humiliating in the very fact that Jael and not Barak himself has killed Sisera (cf. 4:9). As with Sisera, Barak's entry into the tent has a sexual flavor. The Hebrew reports literally, "He went into her, into her tent," doubly emphasizing the sexual implications of each phrase (v. 22). Indeed, the phrase "he went into her" elsewhere in the tradition often precedes the conception of a child (Genesis 30:4–5, 10, 16–17). In this case, however, what emerges from the tent is not a new life, but a corpse (though one birthed, as the poem describes, by a woman): "When he came into her, behold, Sisera lying dead, and the tent peg through his temple." The fact that Jael is anxious to show off Sisera's corpse implies that this proof of her allegiance to Israel was at least part of her motivation. At the same time, the parallel passivity and ignorance of Barak and Sisera underline Jael's even now unknown allegiances. Though the poem may celebrate her as God's warrior, Jael remains in the narrative a loose cannon, a threat to any man who enters her tent.

FRIEND OR FOE, MALE OR FEMALE

In each of the stories under examination here, there is at least a moment when the reader and/or some of the characters wonder, "Whose side is this woman really on?" In Judges 5, as Fewell and Gunn note, the poet obsessively returns to the question of which tribes came out to support the Lord's cause, and which failed to do so.[34]

> ... From Zebulun those who bear the marshal's staff,
> The chiefs of Issachar came with Deborah ...
> Among the clans of Reuben there were great searchings of heart.
> Why did you tarry among the sheepfolds, to hear the piping for the flocks?
> ... Gilead stayed beyond the Jordan,
> and Dan, why did he abide with the ships?
> Judges 5:14b–17a

The final, celebratory lines of the poem underline exactly the issue of allegiance, friend vs. foe:

> So may they perish, all your enemies, YAHWEH!
> But may those who love you be like the rising sun in its strength!

For the poet of Judges 5, Jael's murder marks the boundary between God's friends and enemies. Sisera dies as Yahweh's enemies should—presumably in that his murder shames him even as it kills him. Jael, again presumably, since she has been praised above all other women in previous verses, is counted among "those who love you," and receives their blessing.

But in the story the border between God's own and his enemies is not so clear. At the opening of the prose account we do not know which one Jael is—enemy or lover? Friend or foe? Even her ethnicity, which should give us some clue, is a blank, as though her gender had erased or eclipsed it. Indeed, her gender has eclipsed it in a sense, since it is because she is a woman that we know only her husband's ethnicity and loyalties. Her own are hidden in his—perhaps purposefully, so that she can approach Sisera as a friend. Jael is, it seems, constituted by her gender alone—thus the emphasis on her tent, the connotations of birth, on sex and penetrability—all extremely conventional associations surrounding femaleness in this culture. At the same time, she is busy hiding, and hiding also seems to be a woman's job—hiding Sisera from his enemies as he supposes, hiding him in her tent under more than one covering, hiding her intentions from Sisera and the reader until they are accomplished. Even then, although Jael proudly displays her handiwork to Barak, although it is the subject of song and story, Sisera's dead body never sees the light of day. Once he enters "into her, into the tent," Sisera never, as far as we hear, comes out. Nailed to the female earth, part of the female tent, Sisera dies in a man's nightmare—lured in by shelter and nourishment, he dies imprisoned in, perhaps eaten by, a woman's womb.

So perish all your enemies, YAHWEH, responds the singer of Judges 5. But then, we never see Barak leave Jael's tent either. His entry closely parallel to that of his counterpart and enemy, Barak also enters Jael's tent at her insistence, never to be seen emerging. Surely Barak is not also Yahweh's enemy, though he may have taken a little too long to respond to Deborah's urging. Clearly he is not Jael's enemy. And yet, her tent has become a dangerous place, and a woman who kills is a dangerous thing. One never knows whom her tent will consume next. In the song's simpler view, Jael is for God and thus she is good. No doubt the reassuring quality of that assessment is part of the reason that the poem has the last word. In the received text, the poem's celebration of victory and sorting out of sides quiets the disturbing questions of gender, violence, and loyalty raised by the narrative.

On one level, both story and poem seem written to say to its readers, "Even our women are more manly than their men," and, "more manly, even, than some of our own." Such statements, like Barak's loss of honor at having Sisera killed by a woman, would not loosen traditional roles, but constitute another, somewhat unusual way of reaffirming them. But on another level, the narrative, once immersed in issues of gender and otherness, shakes up the boundaries in such a way that they cannot be easily put back into place. For good or ill, the story makes the woman's tent a public space, where the history of Israel is decided. The woman within is momentarily visible, even while covered and covering; her covering itself is visible. Perhaps, as Fewell and Gunn maintain, this glimpse of patriarchy behind the scenes is necessary for the realism of the overall story:

> After all, no one would believe a story in which no women appeared. Better to reveal a few, lest others grow suspicious that this story might not be representing the truth. Nevertheless, all things considered, it is far better to keep as many of these women as possible under "wraps."[35]

Yet in this particular story, it is Sisera who is literally under wraps, and Jael who covers him, a fact that indirectly seems to threaten Barak as well. There is a sense then, in which the story represents not only a male writer's view of one woman's actions, but a male writer's view of what is required to be a woman—not in its representation of Jael, but in its representation of Sisera. Frightened and rendered helpless by the dangers outside, he is covered, secured, and then crushed by his very protector; this indeed is patriarchy's modus operandi. Accidentally, perhaps, the text in feminizing Sisera and giving Jael masculine qualities seems to expose the very process by which women are controlled and often destroyed. Perhaps it is to be expected that the horrors of rape only truly surface in the biblical text when the rapist is a woman and the victim a man.

REFLECTION QUESTIONS:

1. Heber, Jael's husband, appears to be "missing in action." Why do you think he placed his wife in danger?

2. Why do you think a brave, brilliant warrior like Sisera made such a poor decision by placing his safety and security in the hands of a strange woman?

3. Why do you think Jael provided milk for Sisera when he requested water?

4. Which of the possible motives for the murder seems most plausible to you? What difference does this make in your understanding of the story?

— TWO —

JUDITH

Keeping Kosher with a Vengeance

(READ THE BOOK OF JUDITH IN THE
APOCYPHA)

DAUGHTER OF SIMEON,
AVENGER OF DINAH

SURPRISINGLY, JUDITH'S STORY opens with her genealogy.
Given the intense (if at times conflicted[1]) patrilineal
nature of the biblical tradition, the genealogy of a woman is
almost a contradiction in terms. Daughters are mentioned
only incidentally and occasionally in the biblical text, as they
do not promote the family line into which they are born.
Furthermore, a patrilineal system would be even less interested in who Judith's father was after she married. Becoming
part of her husband's household at marriage, she technically
remains so even as a widow. Hence the plot of Genesis 37 and
of the book of Ruth, where not only are the widows still part
of the dead men's family, they are responsible for its survival.

Judith's connection to this genealogy, and a further emphasis upon it, emerges when she herself invokes the God of her
ancestors. While readers of the Bible are familiar with its
heroes calling upon the God of Abraham, Isaac, and Israel (see
for example Gen. 31:42; Exod. 3:15–16; Jos. 24:2; 1 Kings
8:36; 1 Chron. 29:18), Judith's plea is to the God in particular of Israel's son, Simeon, the avenger of Dinah's rape and, by
happy coincidence, her forefather.

By reminding the reader of Dinah's rape and identifying
God as the avenger of rape, Judith seems on the one hand to
authenticate her femaleness; this appears to be a woman's
view. Her description of the rape seems exceptionally focused
on the woman's body and experience.

> Lord God, the father of Simeon, into whose hand you put a
> sword to avenge the foreigners who criminally loosed the
> womb of the virgin and stripped her thigh shamefully and
> desecrated her womb in disgrace. For you said, "Thus it will
> not be," and they did it. (Judith 9:2)

Yet, as in Genesis, the offended brothers quickly overshad-
ow Dinah's pain, and the prayer becomes an almost poetic,
exultant recital of the ensuing bloodbath.

> Therefore you handed their rulers over to murder, and over
> to blood the bed, which had known the deception that they
> deceived. You struck the slaves together with their rulers, and
> the rulers upon their thrones. Their wives you handed over
> to plunder, and their daughters to captivity, and all their spoils
> to division among the sons beloved by you, who burned with
> your zeal, and they abhorred the defilement of their blood,
> having called upon you for help.

Dinah's virginity has become simply an extension of the
bodies of the brothers; her rape is described in terms that
exclude the girl herself—it becomes "the defilement of their
blood." The offense against the brothers as male guardians of
their sister's virginity thus constitutes the crime both in
Genesis and in Judith's invocation, so that Judith's retelling is
consonant with Simeon's own after-the-fact defense, "Should
our sister be treated like a whore?" (Gen. 34:31). Judith even
celebrates the capture and implicitly the rape of the enemy's

wives and daughters as part of Simeon's revenge. Tellingly, Dinah herself is nameless in Judith's reference; she is simply "the virgin." The initial description of the girl's stripped body comes to seem voyeuristic, given the subsequent erasure of her experience. At least in Genesis, she had a name and a momentary agency—"Dinah . . . went out to visit some of the women of the land" (Gen. 24:1)—before she was completely trampled by brothers and rapists.

With the reference to God giving the sword into the avenging agent's hand (Jdt. 9:2), we are clearly meant to anticipate the sword God puts into Judith's hand and to compare it with that of her forefather. The very fact that we are told Judith's genealogy, leading back to Simeon and thus to Israel, seems largely intended to evoke comparison between Judith and Simeon.[2] Yet, other than being accomplished with the sword, how do they compare? Simeon kills for vengeance because his sister has been raped—vengeance for the shame that Shechem brought Simeon's family. Simeon is a man avenging the rape of a woman. Judith, on the other hand, is a woman, and no one has been raped. There has been neither literal nor metaphorical rape—the penetration of the nation—yet. Judea has not been entered, but is in danger of being, and it is clear that such a penetration will mean desolation; the destruction of the temple and of Jerusalem, the kind of desolation that always follows biblical rape (Jdt. 3:8, 4:2). Similarly, Judith herself is never raped, but only, like Jael, theoretically vulnerable to rape, when she enters the enemy camp and Holofernes's tent.

In fact, Judith seems to be justifying her actions ahead of time by presenting them to God and the reader as vengeance for rape that *might* occur. The similarity here to Judges 5 is striking. There, the imagined response of Sisera's mother as well as some of the details of the narrative scene in Jael's tent assures the reader that Sisera and his men were intent on rape, and that Jael was likely to have been raped had she not lashed out with her pre-emptive strike. Here in Judith's story, though, Judith evokes Dinah's rape to emphasize her own vulnerability and that of the nation. Notably, Judith refers to Dinah's humiliation at the hands of "foreigners" (*allogeneis* 9:2), though in Genesis, Shechem and his people fit no known definition of foreigners. Rather, Judith's own enemies are the foreigners, the Assyrians seeking to loose the womb and expose the thighs of Judea. In fact the same word, *allogeneis,* is used in a Temple inscription forbidding entrance to foreigners.[3] The feared invasion of the city and desecration of the temple become analogous (not for the first time) to the virgin's rape. Judith will return to the theme of the rapes that would have been in her triumphal song: "He threatened to . . . seize my virgins as spoil" (16:4). Thus Judith's actions, which otherwise might seem to be aggression, become entirely defensive and, in particular, a defense against rape. When she is finished praying, Judith will ready herself and enter the enemy camp to kill. But like Jael's, her act of penetration becomes a kind of reverse rape, which is justifiable according to the text on the threat of rape implied by the circumstances.

KEEPING CROSSED BOUNDARIES INTACT

Like Jael again, Judith also lives in a tent. Somewhat eccentrically, she makes a point of living in a tent on the roof of a perfectly good house. The tent-dwelling seems to be part of her ascetic widowhood, which includes refusing all suitors and a great deal of fasting. She fasts "all the days of her widowhood," except for religiously appointed days—the Sabbath, the new moon, and feast days (8:6). Amy-Jill Levine reads the specified days for eating to mean that Judith is "no fanatical ascetic," but a very observant widow who eats and fasts appropriately.[4] But her pattern of fasting outside of religious meals essentially means that Judith is not ruled by her appetites; indeed, she is not said to have any. Eating for Judith is always a religious act; every time she eats, it is an act of religious piety. She eats to keep the law, apparently, on occasions when food is more or less prescribed. The tent, the widowhood, the later refusal of suitors, and the fasting set her apart from the general populace, as Levine notes.[5] Generally, to fast is to take a step away from the society with whom one would normally eat. Eating together strengthens or even creates the bonds of the community; fasting alone conversely delivers Judith into solitude, where she is apparently quite comfortable. It is perhaps less of an effort for her than it would be for others, then, to keep strictly kosher while she is in Holofernes's camp. She is used to eating or not eating by her own religious clock and not by the customs that surround her. And after all, she hardly eats in any case. So we can believe her when she tells Holofernes, "As your soul lives, my lord, your servant will not use up the things I have with me before the Lord carries out by my hand what he has determined to do" (12:4).

Nevertheless, food is part of Judith's arsenal. Despite the tight control on, or absence of, her own appetites, the problem Judith is there to solve is one of hunger and, most directly, thirst. Because the Babylonians have cut off access to all the streams going into the city of Bethulia, the people are all dying of thirst and also hunger, as the lack of water kills off livestock and crops. Thus, Holofernes believes Judith's lie that the people are so hungry, they are on the brink of eating unclean animals, as well as food set aside for sacrifice at the temple (11:12–13). What the people are actually on the brink of, of course, is surrender to these invading Gentile hordes. In a sense, then, what Judith says is true, for surely if Holofernes conquers their city, the survivors will be reduced to eating non-kosher food. Since Bethulia's defenses are, in this story, the last, best hope of Jerusalem, it is also true that if Holofernes razes Bethulia, the first fruits offerings, lacking a temple at which to be sacrificed, will become mundane food.

The story is exceptionally concerned, in fact, with keeping kosher and all that keeping kosher implies within the anthropology of religion. Mary Douglas brought home to biblical scholars the symbolism inherent in food and purity restrictions and the analogy between concern about what enters and exits the body, and concern about maintaining the boundaries of the community.[6] Judith becomes a textbook example of this analogy, since anxiety about Assyrian invasion runs the plot, while strict observance of food regulations permeates the story. In both cases, the issue seems to be the crossing and maintaining of boundaries—specifically the crossing of the other's boundaries while maintaining one's own.

Like Jael, Judith's first act is to invite men into her tent. The similarity ends there, as Judith's invitation resembles a summons more than a seduction and is done by proxy through her maid. Uzziah and the other elders simply "come" to Judith, never explicitly entering her tent at all (8:11). Once Judith has given them a talking to, she leaves the tent, and never, as far as we know, returns. While Jael conducted her business within the boundaries of her tent, Judith goes out to meet Holofernes in his tent, invading rather than being invaded, crossing all walls and guards in between.

And walls and guards there are. Judith asks special permission for Bethulia's city gate to be opened so that she can go out, crossing her own city's anxiously guarded boundary. With her beauty and wisdom she then so amazes the Assyrians at their outpost that they admit her into the territory of their camp and then into Holofernes's tent themselves

(10:15, 20). Again, after her initial conference with Holofernes, servants lead her "into the tent" where she will sleep. From there, at midnight, she sends out to again get special permission to go out of the tent and the camp, to "the wadi of Bethulia," a liminal place between the boundaries of the camp and the city, where, ever wary of contamination, she purifies herself before returning to the tent she has been given.

Judith's crossings emphasize at once the degree to which the story is rife with boundaries and limitations, and the degree to which Judith transcends them. The people of Bethulia are trapped within the city walls without water, while Judith nightly bathes. The Assyrians will allow no Bethulians to leave the city, and the city leaders would like to prevent the Assyrians from coming in, so the wall is guarded and watched from both sides. Just as its own walls are guarded, though, Bethulia as a whole stands guard outside the boundaries of Jerusalem, which in turn acts as a wall of defense before the temple. The story turns upon the fear that if the Assyrians enter Bethulia, Jerusalem will be invaded and the temple desecrated. Bethulia stands at the entrance to one of the mountain passes through which the enemy might invade Judea, passes as narrow as a hallway, "only wide enough for two abreast" (Jdt. 4:7). Thus Bethulia—whose name resembles the Hebrew word for virgin—constitutes the guard of this opening, an orifice, ultimately, of the temple. Clearly, Assyrian penetration of this narrow passage would constitute their political and religious rape of the nation.

Judith crosses all these borders rather pointedly. That is, the borders are duly noted, but in each case special permission is granted her to transgress them. This ability to walk through walls seems to emanate primarily from her beauty and secondarily from her wisdom, as her wisdom generally plays second fiddle to her beauty in this plot. But it is perhaps her piety, forming in a sense the source of the wisdom and the beauty, that makes her so penetrating.

Before leaving her rooftop or even crossing even the boundary of her tent, Judith prays. For this prayer, in contrast to the adornments that follow it, she strips *(egumosen)* down to the sackcloth around her loins and lies prostrate. Significantly, the very next verse has the nameless virgin Dinah shamefully "stripped" *(egumosan)* by the foreigners. The verb is the same in both cases, but in verse one, Judith is the agent, not the object. At the same time, there is no instance in the canonical literature of a female character putting on sackcloth or praying in this penitential manner.

Tamar, when she is raped, immediately rends her virgin's tunic and puts ashes on her head but does not seek out sackcloth (2 Sam. 13:19). In the Bible, those who put on sackcloth and ashes to pray are not weak women, but challenged men: Jacob (Gen. 37:34), Daniel (9:3), Job (16:15), Mordecai (Est. 4:1–4), Israel's enemies (1 Kings 20:31–32; 21:27) or its rulers, including David (1 Chron. 21:16; 2 Kings 19:1–2), or the people as a whole (2 Sam. 3:31; Neh. 9:1). Sackcloth seems to be associated not only with grief but also with the penitence and humility that accompany a desperate petitioning of God. The bereaved might tear their garments and put ashes on their head—indeed the Assyrians rend their garments when they discover Holofernes's headless body—but those in urgent need of God's help put on sackcloth, with or without ashes, and pray. No woman is said to do the latter—except Judith.

Yet, in the prophets, particularly Jeremiah, the daughters of Israel or Israel as a daughter, are told to put on sackcloth, not to petition God, but to mourn the fate of the nation. "Daughter of my people," Jeremiah exorts, "gird on sackcloth, roll in the ashes . . . for sudden upon us comes the destroyer" (6:26). Again in Chapter 49, the prophet insists,

"Shriek, daughters of Rabbah! Put on sackcloth and mourn . . . for Milcom goes into exile along with his priests and captains. Why do you glory in your strength, your ebbing strength, rebellious daughter?" (vv. 3–4). Similarly, Joel uses the mourning girl as an analogy for the repentance of the people, telling them to "Lament like a virgin girl with sackcloth for the spouse of her youth" (1:8).

The image of a grieving young woman, at once widow and virgin in the Joel passage, appears to encapsulate the desperate grief as well as the humility before God that the audience would feel if they truly understood their own situation. The woman's role, as so often within the prophets and elsewhere, is to index the condition of the people as a whole. My guess would be that presenting a named female character with her body exposed in only sackcloth would have been too shocking an image for the writers of biblical narrative. Possibly, women simply did not put sackcloth on as often as men did. Exposing the woman's body in this way may have been reserved for a statement of extreme conditions.

When they are in dire straits, men like Daniel and Job put on sackcloth and ashes to confess sins known and unknown, personal and national. Much of the effect of the wearing of the desperate garb seems to be the message that they stand (or lie) stripped of all defenses but their confidence in God. For the women in these narratives, this kind of stripped-down humanity would be a little too much humanity for the narratives to bear—man, after all, was understood to be the image of God, while woman was rather a lesser version of man. Hebrew culture covered men's and women's bodies fully, but it covered women's bodies more emphatically, keeping them not only in their clothes but also in their homes. But by presenting an anonymous, abstract daughter or virgin as a metaphor, the prophets used exactly the extreme quality of the image for rhetorical effect.

So Judith, a widow indeed, stripping down to the sack-cloth around her loins in order to pray for her own mission, resembles no female character in the Hebrew Bible, but rather (a) a metaphor of national desperation, and (b) several pious, desperate male characters. Her posture, like that of the male characters who put on sackcloth, evokes her humility as a human being before God. Though she never mentions her own gender as any kind of factor in her relationship with God, she emphasizes this humility in her repeated requests that even she, a widow, be the agent of God's vengeance. In her near-nakedness, she does not mumble or weep like Hannah in the temple, but cries out, even shouting at God. Again, it is the defeated Assyrians who will scream, weep, groan, and howl. Judith's prayer is eloquent and passionate, but not at all out of control.

Though the prayer is long, its duration is the extent of Judith's nakedness, and rising from it, she makes her first passage within her own territory. She goes out of her tent and into her house, which she only ever used for holidays (10:2), and there she dresses up. Clearly, the accoutrements of beauty are not part of the ascetic, tent-dwelling lifestyle. In fact, they are a part of her past, the life she shared with her now-dead husband.

Critics often note Judith's beautification here as a passage from death (sackcloth and widow's weeds) to life (jewels and festive garments). But in a sense, she returns from her life as a widow back to a life that has been dead for her, one she shared with a man now dead. The clothes are described as "the festive garments she had worn while her husband, Manasseh, was living" (10:3). In a sense, the process constitutes a passage from life to death. A widow's mourning attire, after all, signifies in part that she survives the deceased; she lives on despite his death. Putting off her widow's weeds reunites her with her dead husband. But it is appropriate for

Judith to put on dead clothes, given that she does so for the purposes of murder.[7]

Of course, the ointment, jewels, and pretty dresses are a costume. Though she is in fact a pious and ascetic widow, she presents herself as sexually available and interested. The narrative emphasizes Judith's transition, piling on the details of her beautification. She moves first from her tent to her neglected house and there removes garments, bathes, applies ointment, arranges her hair, gets dressed, "chooses sandals" for her feet (implying she has an Imelda Marcos-like array of sandals from which to choose), and puts on every kind of jewelry (again indicating her wealth). All of this methodical preparation is apparently worthwhile, since she then causes both her own people and the Assyrians to marvel at her heightened, now phenomenal, beauty.

Judith is naturally beautiful, but she does not astound the multitudes and stun the enemy without the right outfit. This rare glimpse of a woman becoming by artifice more alluring, and the element of deception involved, implies that women's clothing is by definition a costume, at least when the clothing is not widow's weeds. Here, a woman's efforts to emphasize her own beauty are meant to deceive. The implication, like Judith's sword, cuts two ways. On the one hand, it can be understood as exposing the process by which women are forced to mask—to become something more than they are, or to become something other than they are—in order to function in public. On the other hand, the perhaps more likely implication is that when given free rein, women's beauty will deceive men, distract them, and make them do what is not in their best interests. This is good news for Bethulia and Jerusalem, but bad news for Holofernes, the Assyrians, and men in general.

The beauty that is at once real and a mask opens doors. Remarks on Judith's beauty precede the first several instances of her border-crossing. Uzziah praises her for her wisdom, prudence, and piety before he agrees to open the city gate for her (8:28–31), but when Judith appears at the gate, newly dressed, Uzziah and the elders bless her journey as an expression of their astonishment at her new, heightened beauty. She accepts their adulation and blessing—or brushes it aside, bowing to God rather than to the elders—and then orders them, in effect, to get on with it and open the gate.

> They were very much astounded at her beauty and said to her, "May the God of our fathers bring you to favor and make your undertaking a success, for the glory of the Israelites and the exaltation of Jerusalem." Judith bowed down to God. Then she said to them, "Order the gate of the city opened for me, that I may go to carry out the business we discussed." (10:7b–9)

Holofernes's men seem still more entranced by Judith's face, "which appeared wonderful in exceeding beauty" (10:14). The wording here almost suggests she appears magically more beautiful to them than she really is—which, through her elaborate bathing and dressing process, she does. Again her beauty acts like a password to allow her passage across this border. The Catholic Study Bible gives this section of the text the fascinating subtitle "Judith Captured." She ought to be captured as a Bethulian escaping the city's bounds. But instead of falling into the rough hands of captors, she is received as a welcome guest, as much because of her enchanting Judith-ness as because of her offer to betray her own. She remains entirely in control of her own movements—the opposite of a captive, so that rather than being hauled from one place to another, she is gallantly escorted. The Assyrians escort her toward and then into Holofernes's tent. Servants will later escort her into its inner room, and then into her own tent.

Holofernes's reaction to Judith is in some ways a slow motion version of the others' reactions—entranced by her beauty, he willingly lets her in. Alone among the men who crowd the story, Holofernes cherishes a hope if not a certainty that he will get to sleep with this apparently perfect and sexually available woman. While the narrative presents Holofernes as intent on sex and only implies the possibility of rape, cultural critic Margarita Stocker assures us that Holofernes "will certainly resort to rape if his seduction techniques fail."[8] His hope, however, while it says something about his position of power relative to the other characters, ultimately marks Holofernes out as the story's greatest fool. Anyone who thinks they are going to cross Judith's boundaries has another (sharp) thing coming.

DEADLY MEAL, NOT SHARED

When Holofernes invites Judith to join him for a meal, explicitly intending to have her for dessert, she somehow manages to give him the sense that she joins him in the feast while still eating and drinking nothing but her own food. The fact that she only appears to be eating and drinking in communion perfectly reflects her position and anticipates her chastity in the face of the general's lust. Though she has transgressed all set boundaries, Judith keeps her own perfectly intact. Jael may remain forever under shadow of suspicion that she slept with the enemy in order to subdue him, but no such suspicion can rest on Judith. She will not join with him in food or sex, she will not go to bed with him, she will not become one with him in any way. Holofernes's conviction that she will—or even that he will rape her if she does not—reflects nothing more than his foolish and complete misjudgment of her. Judith's terrific care about what she puts in her mouth, or any other orifice, contrasts beautifully with the lascivious but unconscious general, passed out from having drunk more wine than ever before in his life.

Levine's remark that "the Assyrian camp is the realm of the dead"[9] proves particularly interesting in light of Judith's refusal to eat the camp's food. Like Persephone in Hades, Judith must not share the native delicacies, for fear that to do so will make her one of them. Like Persephone's, Judith's free passage in and out of the "realm of the dead" seems linked to what she eats and what she does not. "I will not eat of them," she tells Holofernes as he puts food and drink in front of her, "in order that it not be an offense [*skandalon*]" (12:2).

The Assyrian food and drink seems more than unclean, almost a danger to her, as though eating it might not only be a sin, but cause her to sin. Letting the foreign food enter her body might make her vulnerable to other breeches of her staunchly defended integrity. And if Judith's boundaries break down, all the boundaries that culminate in the temple's walls are in danger. Certainly, consuming the food and wine has the effect on Holofernes of leading to a most dramatic breach in his physical integrity.

During the meal they do not exactly share, Holofernes seems not to care that Judith drinks her own wine. Rather, he extremely enjoys the meal and its promise of impending intimacy—and indulges in the wine of promise so much as to invalidate the promise itself. Both he and his servant, Bagoas, urge Judith to drink. The fact that of the two men urging her to drink the wine of seduction, one is a eunuch, does not bode well for Holofernes's own masculinity.[10] At their insistence, Judith drinks, though without ill effects. We have already seen that Judith is immune to food and drink, among other things. Back in Bethulia, she fasts while the people starve and bathes while they die of thirst.[11] Neither the scarcity of Bethulia nor the plenty of Holofernes's table appear to apply to her.

Assured by her willingness to drink (her own wine) that he will by agreement or by force have sex with her later, Holofernes himself drinks so much that he is rendered incapable of sex, rape, or anything else. More than any of the other men in these stories, Holofernes puts himself completely at the mercy of the heroine. Judith is portrayed as saving Bethulia and Israel by her cleverness and beauty, but in fact the unconscious, helpless state in which Holofernes is killed is not exactly attributable to either. Or is it? He is so charmed by her, the text tells us, that he overdoes it (12:20). He enjoys the promise of her so thoroughly that it goes to his head—literally. The idea that she will sleep with him is equated with both her beauty and the wine; enjoying the wine is enjoying the sense of drinking the wine with her, as the opening interlude of the sex to come. Is this his stupidity, or the power of her beauty? She later tells the elders of the city, "It was my face that tricked him to his destruction" (13:16). Like the sirens luring sailors to their doom, Judith seems to lure Holofernes by her very being to come to her by means of the wine, the very means of his destruction. Thus Stocker concludes that in desiring her, Holofernes desires his own death.[12]

Having anesthetized him, Judith kills Holofernes with the sword "hanging over his bed"—penetrating and symbolically castrating him with the symbol of his own sexuality. Here as in the Judges story, the killing is a masculine act. All Judith's graceful entries and border-crossings seem to have been only previews for this final penetration with the sword. Judith seizes Holofernes's own masculinity to do it, almost as if he were killing himself. And indeed, it was his own sexuality that led him to make his own killing possible—not only supplying the weapon, but leaving himself vulnerable to it. Judith then places into her food sack the severed head, his removed masculinity perhaps, now become kosher itself in that it has been slaughtered, cut, prepared in a manner fitting in the eyes

of the Lord. The story's preoccupation with laws of kashrut is
to some extent explained thusly: Holofernes's death is not
murder, but kosher slaughter.

Yet, as Levine notes, the act is pointedly not kosher slaughter in that Judith has no priestly authority from which she
would be excluded as a woman, and in that the text goes out
of its way to say that she strikes Holofernes twice. A kosher
sacrifice would entail only one blow, a fatal one, but Judith's
requires two. Is this detail meant to indicate her female weakness? Or simply to remind us that although her actions may
resemble a priest's in some ways, she is certainly not one?

Though she has been meticulous about keeping clean and
kosher up to the time of the murder, her contact with
Holofernes's decapitated head would surely contaminate
Judith. Blood and dead bodies were two of the most contam-
inating substances in the purity system. Interestingly, she does
not wash this impurity away. Her daily ablutions in the
Assyrians' camp were designed apparently to wash away the
contaminants acquired in casual contact with foreigners. But
after killing a man and handing his head to her maid, Judith
is never said to purify herself, by ablution or sacrifice. Perhaps
in the mind of the story, the only pure Assyrian is a dead
Assyrian. Certainly it is with the murder that any threat to
Judith's bodily integrity, as well as to the integrity of Bethulia,
Judea, Jerusalem, and the Temple, ends. With the threat of
national and personal rape defeated, Judith's emphasis on
maintaining her own bodily boundaries disappears.

FEMININE CUNNING: JUDITH AND DAVID

Judith is an unlikely priest just as she is an unlikely leader and
warrior, and as such she resembles perhaps no biblical figure
so much as the young David. Both Judith and David chastise

their betters for lack of faith in God against Israel's enemies, and both go out single-handed and virtually unarmed against them. Arising from the people whom Israel's leaders are supposed to protect, armed with nothing but courage, piety, and the weapons provided (partly) by nature herself, the emergence of both Judith and David shames their own established leaders even while it defeats the enemy in murderous and humiliating fashion. Stocker, noting that images of David and Judith are often paired in Western art, remarks that, "like the boy David who slew the giant Goliath, Judith is the meek, weak and humble agent pitted against the mighty, for the feebleness of God's instruments insults his enemies' pretensions."[13]

Even the methods of the two unlikely heroes have some resemblance. In both cases, the act of war is the killing of one prominent man by a blow to the head. In both cases, the dead man's head is chopped off with the dead man's own sword, though in David's case, this decapitation happens only after Goliath is dead (1 Sam. 17:51a; Jdt. 13:6). In both cases, the severed head is then put on display (1 Sam. 17:54; Jdt. 14:1), and in both cases, the enemy is so unnerved by this one murder that the threat to Israel's existence disappears (1 Sam. 17:51b; Jdt. 14:16–19). It seems fairly clear that somewhere in the mind of the author of Judith, the literary figures of Jael and Sisera were communing with those of David and Goliath.

Judith seems to resist being categorized with the other women of the Bible, women such as Esther, who uses, according to Benedikt Otzen, "feminine cunning, as do other biblical females: Sarai and Rebekah, Tamar and Bathsheba, Ruth and Abigail."[14] One wonders, first of all, whether there is a qualitative difference between the feminine cunning of these characters, and the perhaps masculine cunning of Abraham, Jacob, Absalom, and, in other stories, David.

Judith uses her beauty as a weapon, but even in this she is perhaps not so very different than David, whose youth and beauty lead Goliath to underestimate him (1 Sam. 17:42). But David's famous first killing differs from Judith's in being his only contact with the enemy; indeed, David only gets close to Goliath after Goliath is dead. Judith's killing is much more elaborately planned, takes much longer, and requires much more proximity to its target, making her that much more vulnerable.

David's defeating Goliath is remarkable for its open antagonism, like that of a football game, with David happily shouting Goliath's doom at him while Goliath laughs and threatens. Judith, on the other hand, because she is a woman and lacks a slingshot, must lie in every sense in order to get close enough to the enemy to use his sword. Feminine cunning is not about the intent to deceive. Most biblical heroes do so intend. The value system of the text, like many contemporary value systems, understands deception as a useful survival strategy, to be employed by the quick-witted against their powerful but pitifully obtuse enemies, represented in figures such as Judith's Holofernes and Esther's Ahasuerus. Feminine cunning, if there is such a thing in the biblical text or elsewhere, is not about intending to deceive, but about the particular tools women must use to accomplish the deception.

JUDITH AS A WOMAN

The fact that Judith uses Holofernes's sword means, among other things, that she has no weapon of her own. Her beauty can gain her entry, can get her out of the city, into Holofernes's camp and his tent, but it cannot penetrate his body or cut off his head. For that, since Judith is not a man, she must pick up a man's weapon. She has to act as a man to kill since, as a woman, the story sees her as incapable of it.

But it is not only this moment of masculine killing that troubles Judith's gender. There are several moments of the story when, despite her beauty and its great charm, her status as female seems to be in question. We have noted several of these along the way. She strips herself to sackcloth and petitions the deity, as only men are known to do in this tradition. Unlike any biblical woman, she has a patrilineal genealogy, though as a woman, she could make no contribution to it. Women's usual contribution to biblical genealogies or biblical narratives is as mother, a vehicle moving the line from father to son. But Judith is childless and unconcerned about that fact, a condition in which we find few other biblical women.

Judith's status as a childless widow makes the story possible, as other critics have noted, since a living husband would have been shamed by her seeming seduction, or even by her leaving the house in those sandals. Stocker goes so far as to say that God has killed Judith's husband because, being a jealous god, he wants her for himself, and Levine notes that no man but the deity appears worthy of Judith.[15] Like the presence of a living husband, the presence of children would hinder Judith's freedom of movement and give her concerns other than the nation's or the temple's survival. More importantly, it would also detract from the aura of virginity that surrounds her despite her marriage, a perpetual impermeability rather like that of the Virgin Mary. Indeed, Judith was read as a type of Mary by medieval and renaissance interpreters. If Mary's other children, mentioned in the gospels, disappeared in the glare of her supernatural virginity, Judith's lack of children does not appear in the story at all, except by implication.

Like Jael, then, Judith is not a mother. Unlike Jael, there is no hint of the maternal in Judith's actions. While Jael provides milk and coverings to the man she will kill and welcomes him into her womblike tent, Judith never gives Holofernes so much as a drop of water. He never comes near her womb or her tent, and she never acts other than as a guest (a rather rude guest, in the end) to him.

In Judith's story it is not the food that she offers, but that which she eats, seems to eat, and does not eat that signifies. She is never a nurturer but always a careful consumer. While Jael nurtures Sisera into his grave, symbolically bringing him "into her" in order to kill him, Judith's task is only to approach Holofernes while maintaining the boundary between herself and him, a boundary outlined in the separation of food and drink, until she can render his boundaries defunct.

INVADERS, WOMEN, AND IMPENETRABILITY

One of the questions facing interpreters of Judith is whether the story is a historical fiction or a fable. Is the story designed to tell us something about an event in the history of Judea/Israel, or is it meant to tell us something more general about the meaning of that history? The enemy in the book of Judith seems to be a combination of two of Israel's greater destroyers, the Assyrians and the Babylonians, brought together here without regard to history, by placing the Babylonian Nebuchadnezzar as the Assyrians' king. The story's placement in time is further confused by the reference to the Jews' recent return to Judea and rebuilding of the temple, which would position these events just after the Babylonian Exile. Yet the Assyrians, who overtook the north and threatened Judea before the rise of Babylon, are the enemy. Either the author is thoroughly confused, or these references are meant to let the reader know that this story is more a distillation of and comment on Jewish history than it is any sort of historical account.[16]

Then there is the character of Judith herself, beginning with her name, meaning, rather generically, "Jewish woman," or possibly "Judean woman." Judith seems, as many have remarked, to represent the nation of Judea if not the people of Israel, to embody them as the nation or the people are often embodied in metaphor, as a woman. A widow, she appears initially alone and in mourning, the picture of the grieving, invaded Judea. Yet, as though that image had sprung to life from its home on a Roman coin, Judith in our story gets up, talks back to her leaders, takes off the mourning clothes, bathes off the ashes, and gets dressed up to go out and take care of business. She is beautiful, wise, and wealthy as the ideal nation would be, and uses all of these attributes in the service of the people. Her courage and piety put her in danger of being raped, invaded by the foreigners, as the resistance of Judea places it in danger of invasion by the same foreigners. When she initially summons the elders, they are called "the elders of her city." There is a sense in both this phrase and in her interaction with the Bethulian elders of Judith that she is proprietress or patron saint of the city, for the most part letting it run itself while she attends to her own piety, but in times of crisis intervening in its defense. In her song of triumph, Judith leads the people, speaking in a voice appropriate to the nation as a whole or even to God:

> [The Assyrian] said he would burn my hills,
> and put my youths to the sword,
> and throw my nursing babies to the ground,
> make my infants prey,
> and take my virgins as spoil. (Jdt. 16:4)

But Levine notes that although the book suggests Judith as a metaphor for the Jewish community, the metaphor crumbles upon examination: "The community is historically active; women per se are not."[17] But Judith is publicly active, calling a council meeting, infiltrating the enemy camp, assassinating Holofernes and instructing others as to how best to display his head so as to reduce the enemy to rubble. Judith, then, is not exactly a woman.

Of course, she is a woman. She is a married and bereaved woman, a widow; she is a seductress; she is beautiful and acts by means of her beauty; all of this entirely fits with the woman's social role. But as Levine also notes, Judith is distanced from other women in several ways. First of all, she is more than they are: more beautiful, wealthier, wiser, more pious, more kosher. In these ways she represents a man's ideal of a woman, a sort of ancient Jewish Barbie doll—rather than a real woman. Secondly, unlike the usual social definition of biblical women, Judith has, as we have noted, no children and no obligation to conceive, carry, care for, or even consider children. We are told that her husband left her servants and servant girls—*paidas* and *paidiskos,* terms that share a root with the Greek word for child: *paidion.* The servants add to her status as an independent woman of means; the presence of children, on the other hand, would connect her bodily to others and imply transgression of her carefully maintained bodily integrity. As Sidnie White Crawford notes, although Judith's situation—widowed while yet childless—would seem to dictate it, the idea of levirate marriage is never mentioned. Unlike most women in the biblical tradition (but like Jael), Judith is unperturbed by her childlessness; she never even seems to notice it.

Feminist readers are cheered by Judith's exemption from the biblical obligations of motherhood and her extraordinary freedom of movement and autonomy. Yet, is this a momentary loosening of the restricting roles and rules of gender? Or is it only that Judith can be trusted with such autonomy because she is not exactly female? Rather, she is a metaphor, incompletely embodied, dressed as a woman.

One of the reasons that the prophets called up images of grieving virgins and desolate whores to describe the condition of Israel was that women were defined as permeable in a way that men were not. The extent to which Israel's boundaries were endangered or had been disregarded could be represented in a woman—a well-protected virgin, a woman in danger of being raped, or a woman shamefully allowing entry to all. In any of these images, the woman is seen as vulnerable to penetration and transgression, as is the nation. In Judith, however, this metaphor becomes confused. On the one hand, she appears to be, like the nation, in danger of being raped. On the other hand, she is so good at maintaining her own boundaries, allowing nothing foreign or profane to cross them, while at the same time she transgresses all other existing boundaries herself, that she comes to seem the exact opposite of the vulnerable, permeable woman. Judith's bodily integrity is like a force field. She takes her own food with her where she goes so that nothing of her surroundings penetrates her. She does not seem to need anything from outside herself, even while she is in Bethulia—thus the lack of water and food there does not affect her at all, and she later refuses all suitors—all the men who dream of crossing her boundaries. Even while she is in Holofernes's camp, the threat of rape seems only theoretical. She has no apparent fear, and when she says exultantly, "I will drink, lord, for my life is magnified in me today more than all the days since I was born!" (12:18) the reader is inclined to believe her. Her enthusiasm for the impending greatness of her deed raises rather the image of a righteous warrior than a possible assault victim.

Judith appears sexually available, not only in her dress-up

clothes but in the fact that she is female. She seems penetrable, as women in the biblical text are understood to be, by definition. But like the clothes, her gender is an illusion. Though her beauty draws men to her, it is an expression of the same piety that serves to keep them away. Judith boasts that it was her beauty (and not her sexuality) that killed the enemy, but Uzziah praises her, "You averted our disaster, walking upright before God." That is, Judith's righteousness, the fact that "she feared God exceedingly," is responsible for Holofernes's death and the salvation of the temple. It is because Judith walked upright before God, then, that she is not raped, Judea is not penetrated, and the temple is not desecrated. Her piety and her impenetrability are the same thing, and both are represented in her beauty and her wisdom. Ultimately, her impenetrability is so consistent and intense as to bring not only her gender but her humanity into question. The people of Bethulia are ready to surrender to the Assyrians because they are hungry and thirsty; Judith does not feel these human needs and is therefore able to defend the city and the nation. Likewise, she feels no need for sex (as witness her refusal to marry) and does not need much in the way of shelter (initially she lives in a tent) or clothing (she wears sackcloth and widow's weeds). Need leaves the people vulnerable to invasion; Judith's lack of need means she is invulnerable, penetrating while not being penetrated, and not entirely human.

Margarita Stocker has amply documented the fascination that Judith held for the Christian West throughout the Middle Ages and Renaissance. Stocker holds Judith to be unique in biblical and Western tradition, as a female figure who acts as a public leader and a warrior. "She was permitted to possess the sexual charisma of a Cleopatra without dying for it," Stocker notes, "as in such tales women customarily do."[18] Yet Judith's legacy of challenge to gender boundaries is mixed. She has been remembered and reinterpreted often in her role as metaphor for the nation. But as a metaphor, she retains the outlines of the masculine imagination from which she sprang, like Athena from Zeus's head, motherless. Like the feminine figure of Wisdom in Proverbs, she is allowed privileges and honor that simply do not apply to real women, even to the more fully embodied female characters of the biblical texts.

REFLECTION QUESTIONS:

1. What role do you play as a woman in your family? church? community? What do you do and/or who do you turn to when you have to make major decisions?

2. To what extent does the character of Judith work as a metaphor for the nation?

3. Have you ever had to beautify yourself to get something done? If yes, how?

4. Today, what garment might you consider as symbolic of sackcloth?

5. Have you ever fasted? If yes, how and for what purpose?

6. Is there such a thing as "feminine cunning"? If so, what is it? Can you think of contemporary examples of it? Does Judith practice feminine cunning, or should we simply say she is clever or wise?

— THREE —

ESTHER

Sleeping (and Drinking) with the Enemy

(READ THE BOOK OF ESTHER)

ENEMIES AND OTHERS

So FAR, THE WOMEN WE HAVE looked at have accomplished their killings with relative speed and admirable simplicity; but not so Esther. To begin with a very basic point of comparison: the story of Esther is longer than either Judith's or Jael's. Disproportionate even to the quantity of text is the quality of additional plot complexities in the book of Esther. Compared to the tales we have looked at so far, Esther's story has more numerous and more developed characters, a significant male ally, and, perhaps most importantly, a more elaborately imagined enemy. In Esther, the issue of "Otherness" rises to new prominence. Esther herself and her uncle and other half, Mordecai, are the Jewish "Others" in a Persian world. They are residents rather than visitors in the enemy camp.

Indeed, the enemy is no longer camping in the book of Esther; rather she and Mordecai are residents in an emphatically established enemy city amid elaborate physical and social structures. In a sense, the two named Jews are Others even within the story, since the story begins in the Persian court without them, as though it were a royal Persian tale into which these two initially powerless Jews have wandered.

"Mordecai and Esther are introduced almost *en passant,*" Bea Wyler remarks, noting that, "Two chapters of the book—one quarter of the whole text—pass before the book 'turns Jewish'."[1]

In Jael's and Judith's stories, the enemy was a military leader, and the encounter took place in a tent near a battlefield. But in Esther's story, the more permanent edifices point to the more permanent connection of the Jews to the Gentiles. Jon D. Levenson notes that the text does not imagine a time or place beyond Jewish life in the Persian empire; places and events in Palestine are more irrelevant here than in any other biblical book.[2] Although Mordecai is said to be an exile, there is no sense in the text that he longs or hopes to return.

Perhaps because the heroine and all the Jews in this story are so much a part of the Others' world, the enemy in Esther is not a passive (sleeping) recipient of her courage and aggression, as we saw with Jael and Judith. Esther's enemy, Haman, awake and aware as he dies, sees his downfall coming, though not at her hands. He is not only conscious but deeply involved in plots of his own, and obsessed with the destruction of a Jew, which necessitates the destruction of all Jews. Indeed, he is aware enough to present to the king a view of the Jews as Other in this Persian world: "Dispersed among the nations throughout the provinces of your kingdom, there is a certain people living apart, with laws differing from those of every other people," he informs the king, and surely this much is true. Yet, far from living apart, Esther at least is living very much within, near to the very heart of the empire. Furthermore, we never see Jewish law running contrary to Persian custom in the book of Esther; in fact, we do not see Jewish law at all.

In the Hebrew version of the text at least, there is no suggestion that either Mordecai or Esther keeps kosher, nor any sense that they are unable as Jews to meet Persian social expectations.[3] Only Mordecai's refusal to bow to Haman brings them into conflict with the Persian establishment, and this refusal occurs for obscure reasons, reasons not obviously related to Mordecai's Judaism. The Jews in the book of Esther are not paying the least attention to their own laws, but like the other characters in the book, they are obsessed with Persian law.

Perhaps, then, Haman is lying about the Jews' law, as he is certainly lying when he says that the Jews "do not obey the laws of the king, and so it is not proper for the king to tolerate them" (3:8). Yet technically, Mordecai's refusal to bow does constitute disobedience to the laws of the king, since the king had in fact ordered it (3:2). Haman's description of the Jews—who were apparently entirely unfamiliar to the king until this point—is then both true and false, at once a statement of the facts and a poisonous and chauvinistic slander. But of course, this is not actually a non-Jewish view of Jews but a Jewish view of what non-Jewish anti-Semites say when there are no Jews in the room. Like Eddie Murphy's famous "White Like Me" skit on *Saturday Night Live,* the scene between Haman and the king is a minority's effort to imagine the majority world that goes on behind their backs, in which the dominant conspire to keep the "Other" suppressed.[4]

The accusations worsen in the decree that Haman convinces the king to write. There the Jews are accused of committing terrible crimes, in addition to living according to their own divergent laws; here at last is an undiluted lie. In the contemporary reader's mind, Haman's accusations may seem rather innocuous. They are most likely understood by the text to be false stereotypes, containing merely a grain of truth—just enough to make them dangerous. Contrary to what Haman says, the Jews are not separate. They do not follow their own laws or refuse to obey the laws of the land. Why, the Jews are hardly even Jewish!

The book is ambivalent about assimilation. It shows no interest in returning to Palestine and apparently approves of Esther's initial silence concerning her origins. Yet Mordecai is continually referred to as "Mordecai the Jew" (5:13, 6:10, 8:7, 9:29), again in a kind of outsider-insider formulation. For who but a gentile would give Mordecai this tag, almost a surname? Mordecai is open about his own ethnicity, and possibly his religion is somehow implied in his refusal to bow to Haman, as the Septuagint version claims.

In the end, the Jews' salvation depends both on Esther's secrecy about her identity and on her later claiming that identity before the king. In order for all the Jews, including Esther, to survive, Esther had to pass as Persian, just as light-skinned African Americans have sometimes passed as white in order to survive racism. Esther passed, as it was called among African Americans, so that she could become queen and win the king's favor. But she also had to choose to use that favor on behalf of her own people, in order for all the Jews, including herself, to survive. Ethnic identity, then, the living connection to one's people, is essential and must be maintained—but to survive, one ought to know when and where to maintain it under wraps.

ONE FOR ALL AND ALL FOR ONE

In fact, the book of Esther continually makes links between the individual and the people whom that individual represents. We see this first when the king's advisors understand Vashti's defiance as potentially leading to a revolution of all women, rising up against the authority of their husbands. Levenson argues that here and elsewhere, Ahasuerus confuses the personal with the political. Vashti's refusal is in his reading personal, a marital dispute and not a matter that legislation can affect. But one need not be deeply committed to feminist theory to see that, like many marital disputes, this one is both personal and political. The king's advisors are not so very wrong, perhaps, in guessing that such insubordination on the part of the queen could loosen the patriarchy's ever-tenuous hold on power. Theoretically, Rosa Parks's refusal to give up her seat on the Alabama bus was based on a very personal weariness, but certainly it had immediate, widespread political implications. Every society intends such refusals of cooperation to seem impossible, even inconceivable; when one happens, observers find themselves peering through a door of possibility into an altered social world.

It is also true, as Levenson may be hinting, that even if an individual's action does not effectively threaten, those in power might nevertheless imagine it to do so. That is, the example of one individual, particularly a prominent one, challenging the status quo can easily be perceived by those invested in the status quo as a serious threat, whether or not it was intended as such. So, for example, the fictional pregnancy of the unmarried television character Murphy Brown was seen by then Vice President Dan Quayle as a threat to the whole national social structure, though others interested in making changes to the social structure perceived no such effect. Defenders of the present power structures often feel that they are under siege, so that they come to perceive what might be intended as personal or offhand as an intentional political challenge. Had Dan Quayle had the legislative power of Ahasuerus, or the influence of Memucan, no doubt American television would look very different today.

Vashti is understood by the king's advisors to stand for all women, or at least for all wives. Their response to her individual act is to deal with her individually and also with women in general, by means of law. At the advice of Memucan, the king issues a law forbidding Vashti to come into his presence and deposing her from the queenship, then writes a letter to all the provinces demanding that men should rule in their own homes. He thus disposes of Vashti's insubordination and pre-emptively shuts down any other insubordination it might inspire.

The brevity of Vashti's story invites interpreters to see it as insignificant. Levenson rather vehemently denies Vashti's importance, noting disapprovingly that, "some may wish to make of her a feminist heroine. The narrator, however, has no interest in her after this brief passage."[5] But if the narrator has no further interest in her, I do. She may indeed be merely a plot contrivance meant to clear the position of queen for Esther. Yet for this purpose any of a number of different plots could have been contrived; the author chose to create an insubordinate, banished first queen, rather than have the king's first wife, say, die in her sleep or run off with one of the many courtiers. Levenson himself notes the counterpoint that Vashti provides for Esther:

> Queen Vashti's absolute and uncompromising refusal to com-
> ply with her husband renders her powerless and ineffective
> and ultimately sweeps her from the scene. The positive
> antipode to her is Esther, who because she maintains relations
> (in both the sexual and general sense) with Ahasuerus, is able
> to gain power and to achieve goals higher than the mainte-
> nance of her own dignity.[6]

Vashti's presence in the narrative does then say something about gender and power after all. At the same time, the counterpoint of Vashti's defiant refusal to enter versus Esther's manipulative entry and work from within is complicated by the presence of Mordecai in the story. For if Vashti's "absolute and uncompromising refusal to comply . . . renders her powerless," how are we to view Mordecai's similar refusal? If Esther is Vashti's positive antipode where gender relations are concerned, surely she is Mordecai's positive antipode where Jewish-Gentile relations or ethnic politics are concerned. Levenson seems to view concern for one's own dignity as petty when he sees it in Vashti, but not to notice it in Mordecai.

In the Hebrew text, our best guess as to why Mordecai will not bow is that he is primarily concerned with his personal dignity. Though the Greek additions have Mordecai insisting to God, "I will not bow down to anyone but you, my Lord" (Esther 3:2), no such motivation is offered in the Hebrew. The addition in the Greek of this religious motivation to Mordecai's defiance serves indeed to point out early readers' discomfort with the text as it stood. For, if Vashti's refusal results in her own banishment and a reinforcement of male rule, Mordecai's refusal is poised to result in his own death and the death of all the Jews. Esther's ancient readers were no doubt disturbed that a text that seems so interested in diaspora survival strategies would hold up as a model an act that, by its own account, endangers the entire group.

By Chapter 3 then, in the position formerly held by an openly defiant woman is the secretly Jewish woman, Queen Esther, who is secretly related to and advised by an openly defiant Jew. Vashti's strategy is not available to her, since for the sake of the Jews, Esther will need the access to the king that Vashti both refuses and loses. Similarly, Esther will gain proximity to the king by doing as Mordecai says but not as he does—by hiding her identity and being notable for her compliance. Unlike Vashti or Mordecai, Esther works from within the system.

SEX, BOOZE, AND BOUNDARY CROSSING

Yet inside the outsiders' realm, as we will see, there is within and then there is within; there are levels of proximity to the throne, and each level is fenced and guarded. Despite her permanent status in the Other's kingdom, boundary crossings remain key to Esther's story. Vashti's would-be crossing from her own banquet and a woman's world, into the masculine world of the king's banquet is the first of these, and signals how significant boundaries will be for the plot. In retribution for her refusal to cross this boundary at the king's command, Vashti is commanded never again to cross it—she will come when the king calls, or not at all. This same boundary will plague Esther's story, but in reverse—as queen, Esther desires entry when the king has not called. But Esther must cross several boundaries before she becomes queen.

Men and women are sharply segregated in this text, in a way that ethnic groups are not. Only men are present in the king's court and at several of his banquets, and only women are at Vashti's banquet or, of course, in the harem. Men do not go to the women's space for any reason, and when women emerge into the presence of men, they need a eunuch, or several, to shuttle them across the boundary. As the eunuchs do not fit squarely into either gender category, the text presumably understands them as particularly adept at navigating the spaces in between.

Indeed, it is a eunuch who brings Esther into her proximity to the king in the first place, though this position is initially a dubious honor. Neither Mordecai nor Esther shows any sign of wanting Esther to become queen. Mordecai's advice to her not to reveal her ancestry may be designed to facilitate her selection from the other virgins, or it may be in the interests of Esther's safety. For the contest is perilous. The girls are "gathered" from the countryside, with or without their or their families' consent. It is difficult to imagine any family would have given consent, had they been asked, since while the departing girl would have a slim chance to become queen, she had a much better chance of being tried and discarded, whereupon she would be returning to her home, should she make it there, no longer a virgin and so no longer marriageable. The precarious position of the girls is underlined by Mordecai's daily inquiries at the harem entrance as to Esther's well-being (2:11).

Like Judith, Esther is naturally beautiful but nevertheless goes through elaborate beautification procedures, which, as they did for Judith, facilitate her passage across the crucial boundaries. Both stories make it clear that to please men requires artistry. Indeed, Esther and all the virgin candidates for queen go through a full year of being bathed, perfumed, and possibly trained. Esther then has the additional and apparently indispensable help of the eunuch Hegai, which includes the provision of seven maids, the right foods, and the best living quarters in the harem (2:9). She wins the king's favor not only because she is naturally beautiful but because she was Hegai's best student; pleasing the king, or by extension any man, is a hard-won accomplishment.

Among those who strive—whether willingly or because they have no other choice—for this achievement, anxiety is high. Each girl, approaching her audition night, is permitted to take whatever she wants with her from the harem into the palace, from the women's space into the men's (2:13). On the one hand, this permitted accoutrement has the status almost of weapons or armor, tools with which the girls may hope to win some position at court. Thus, Esther's decision to take nothing with her except what Hegai recommends, recalls David's choice to face Goliath without armor or sword.

At the same time, I have learned from my children that frightening transitions are made easier by the presence of objects taken from the former condition into the latter—so my sons insist on taking a toy or book or even a piece of construction paper from home to school, and beg to bring the school toys or even their classmates home. The allowance for accompanying objects in Esther seems designed to ease the transition; yet the very necessity of easing it points out to the reader just how treacherous that transition is. The fact that Esther takes with her only what Hegai recommends signifies therefore confidence in her own pleasing ability to navigate from here to there, as well as her confidence in the navigating abilities of her guide.

Every girl "would go in the evening and return in the morning to a second harem under the care of the royal eunuch Shaashgaz, custodian of the concubines. She could not return to the king unless he was pleased with her and had her summoned by name" (2:14). When Esther goes to the king, however, it initially seems as though she will return neither to the first nor to the second harem. Rather, having won the king over at once and been crowned queen on the spot, she seems to be whisked off directly to the royal banquet in her honor. Yet the next time we hear about her relationship to the court, Esther is telling Mordecai that she has not been summoned to the king for thirty days (4:11). When the banquet was over, it seems, Esther was put back on a shelf, not unlike the women who failed to win the king's favor.

In fact, being queen does not seem to have improved Esther's access to the throne very much. While she was a relatively undistinguished virgin, she waited in the harem for the king to summon her. Now that she is queen, she is still there—in some version of a harem—waiting for the king's summons. Her wording to Mordecai, that "any man or woman who goes to the king without being summoned suffers the penalty of death" (4:11), places Esther herself as one among many of the king's underlings, courtiers, concubines, and wives, all of whom might need access to him but must wait upon his whim.

Her ability to break or transcend this law is not based on her position as queen—like others, the queen takes her life in her hands by going to the king uninvited. Rather, she crosses that deadliest of boundaries by virtue of her singular ability to please, and by virtue of the king's sexually symbolic scepter, extended to meet her suggestive touch. That is, she crosses into the arena of power now in the same way that she became attached to it originally, through her ability to make the king desire her sexually.

The sexual act is notably absent—at least explicitly—from the account of Jael's sedation of Sisera, and Judith explicitly exults, "he committed no act of sin with me, to defile and shame me." Despite the sex in the air, despite the sex in the food and drink, it is important that these women not sleep with the man they are cozying up to, because it is important that despite appearances, they are not indeed communing with, or becoming one with the enemy. Esther, on the other hand, eats and drinks with Ahasuerus and the evil Haman, and why not? After all, she is already in bed with the gentile king, at least occasionally.

In a sense, Haman's approach to Esther's couch and the accusation of attempted rape follows up on Esther's already being compromised in marriage to a gentile, albeit a gentile king. Somewhere in the unconscious of the story is perhaps the sense that since Esther sleeps with the gentile king, why not with the gentile king's Jew-hating advisor; why not with her cousin's would-be hangman; why not with the very author of her people's destruction? After all, she is already pleasing Haman with food and drink. After all, the author of the decree to destroy the Jews is not finally Haman at all, but the king himself, Esther's husband and lover.

While Jael provides for but does not share with Sisera, and Judith simply eats and drinks alongside Holofernes, Esther eats with the king and Haman not once but twice, at her own insistence. She does not keep kosher, and indeed the book of Esther is as unconcerned with keeping kosher as the book of Judith is concerned. Rather, Esther's sharing two meals with the enemy underlines how involved she is with "them," the people who are endangering her own. Her identity as one of the "us" in the story is indeed as much a voluntary act for her as a condition of existence. In the meals themselves, Esther appears wholly identified with the Persian court, largely, as Timothy Beal notes, through the medium of wine.

In the book of Esther, Beal observes, "the place and time for drinking is also often the place and time for defining 'us' over against 'them,' and for consigning 'them' to oblivion."[7] Likewise, Michael V. Fox notes that the banquets are continually the "vehicle for the theme of power—its gain and its loss."[8] We see here, perhaps, some of what the author of Judith draws upon, in that Esther's success, like Judith's, depends upon her ability both to please the man in charge and to get him drunk. In the book of Esther, as in Judith, pleasing him, sleeping with him, and getting him drunk are all closely tied, if not equated.

In this story where laws abound and everything is legislated, one notable exception is the wine. In fact, the wine as an exception to the legislation is itself legislated in the king's second banquet (which follows hard on the first): "And the drinking by command was not compelled, for so the king instructed all of the wine stewards of his palace, to serve each man as he wished" (1:8). The edict from the king appears to be that this is an all-you-can-drink affair, a bottomless cup, an open bar; overindulgence is not required by law, but it need not be; given the opportunity to drink as they please for free, we can assume that the courtiers are getting almost as drunk as is the king himself. As Lillian Klein remarks, the king appears to have given up his control over the guests where their drinking is concerned, and to have invited them in turn to give up their self-control.[9] Food, on the other hand, is notable for its absence from this initial, detailed description, a description so vivid and lavish that it colors our sense not only of the banquet it describes, but of each of the eight banquets that follow before the book of Esther comes to an end. Everything from the guest list to the materials used for the curtains is described in great detail, with particular attention to the drinking vessels and the wine (1:6–8), but there is no mention of actual nourishment. Klein notes that the meal seems initially to be a redistribution banquet, in which the king's subjects taste the benefits of his prosperity, but all that is being redistributed is the wine and its accompanying drunkenness.[10]

Bodily fluids are carriers of contamination in the biblical purity system. The fluidity of wine seems to evoke the kind of connection or contagion that the purity system keeps in check. In Judith, we saw that drinking together seems to be understood by Holofernes as sexual in itself. Judith thus refuses to share wine or sex, nearly in the same gesture. The absence of any reference to the purity system in Esther may not indicate a lack of consciousness of it, but rather a sense that it cannot be maintained. Then as now, the drinking party operates as an informal and unpredictable but fertile and lively matrix for the exchange of power. The party in this story is a liminal space, outside of law and consequently able to compose, if not to erase laws. It is invariably at banquets that, as Fox puts it, "the will of others becomes law."[11] In the fluid lawlessness of the wine, it seems, a drinking partner's desire passes into the king and thence into law. In the book of Esther, laws emerge invariably from the chaos of the unlegislated.

Sex shares wine's immunity to and transcendence of law, so that women only cross into the men's world when the king desires them. The pleasure of wine and the pleasures of sex appear in fact to stand in for one another. As Judith's presence and sexual promise are enough to cause Holofernes to drink himself into unconsciousness, so Esther's sexual connection to the king enables her to draw him into (more) drinking. For his extension of the scepter to her results in his foolishly generous offer to grant her every wish, and the wish she expresses is simply to serve him wine. Or rather, to serve him and Haman wine, in the privacy of her own quarters.

The fact that Esther is actually sharing the wine, so to speak, with the king points to another difference between her story and Jael's or Judith's. Esther's being legitimately and thoroughly in bed with the king means she is a queen and not a warrior. After murdering Sisera, Jael can run to the general of the Israelite army to show him her good deed; Judith can return triumphant to Bethulia, with the enemy's head in her hand—but the enemy camp is Esther's home. Even Abigail, though she is like Esther married to the problem, can use her powers of feeding and seduction to defeat the marriage; like Judith and Jael, Abigail lands at last under the rule and in the territory of the people of God. But while Esther can rejoice with Mordecai and the Jews when Haman is executed and the Jews take up arms, she remains at the story's end in her perhaps duplicitous role as the gentile ruler's hostess, lover, and servant—a role that was a one-night stand for Jael and for Judith. The killings that Jael and Judith commit are acts of war, in a context of war. Esther's story, however, is not about war but court intrigue. The enemy here is a rival for influence over the king. While the deaths of Sisera and Holofernes meant freedom and sovereignty for Israel, Haman's death simply means that the Jews can survive and the status quo can continue.

The problem in the story is not that the king is a bad man or even that he is easily manipulated. The problem is that the king is being manipulated by the wrong advisor. The purpose of Esther's banquet is not to kill the king or his advisor but to manipulate the king, redirect his killing power, so that "the sword hanging over his bed" becomes metaphorical rather than literal. Esther's aim and the hope of the Jews is not to dismantle the apparatus of power. The apparatus of power, in both its constructive and destructive aspects, in its power both to honor and to shame, remains perfectly intact at the story's end. All that has changed is the position of Esther, Mordecai, and the Jews in relation to it. The gallows, the king's horse and his honorific procession, the king's signet ring, his irrevocable edicts, and the foolish, malleable, drunken power of the king himself all remain intact exactly as they were as the story progresses; what changes is their effect on the protagonists. The royal power forms a kind of permanent, albeit flawed, center around which Jews and Gentiles circle, from the position of winning, honored, and powerful destroyer to that of losing, powerless victim of slaughter, and vice versa.

Esther accomplishes this spin of the wheel of power through the provision of food and, more prominently, drink. When the king asks what she wants the first time, she says that she wants to wine and dine the king and Haman. When Ahasuerus comes to the banquet and drunkenly repeats his promise to give her anything, she again asks to be allowed to entertain him and his advisor. Is she lying about what she really wants? Or is she rather capable at this point only of wanting more contact with these men and their power of destruction, more influence over them to flow from them to her, as the wine flows from her to them? Sisera's basic request for water and Jael's simple opening of a skin of milk are replaced here with a series of complex banquets, requests, and vows. Jael's use of the tool that came to hand is replaced with, well, with Esther's using the tool that came to hand; namely, the king himself.

But while it makes good practical sense that Esther would want to gladden the king's heart with liquor and food before making her true request, the plot does not similarly demand the presence of Haman at the meal. Esther does not need to please or even to appear to please Haman; she simply needs to replace him as the author of the king's laws. Yet she does invite him, with the king, to both of her banquets, and she does please him very much. Indeed, he leaves her first banquet on top of the world, drunk with the light of his own rising star (5:9). The effect of his having dined with Esther, then, is this additional perceived elevation in Haman's status, a side effect of which is that he has a gallows built for Mordecai, whose presence as a fly in the ointment he can no longer tolerate precisely because everything else is going so well. His invitation to and presence at the banquets produces additional irony, then, since the reader knows that Esther's final aim is not to increase Haman's delight.

But these narrative effects do not entirely explain Esther's motivation for inviting him. I would argue that the story perceives a connection between the drinking and the dying that necessitates Haman's presence at a banquet where his downfall will constitute the final course. Critics have long noted that Haman's thriving necessitates Mordecai's downfall and vice versa; indeed, one's life means the other's death. But fewer notice that the same equivalence applies to Esther as well. Her survival is dependent on Haman's destruction and death. The kill-or-be-killed situation is evoked by both Haman and Esther being present at the banquet. Eating, as we noted in the introduction to this volume, is the process of individual and communal life emerging from death. The story of Esther connects most powerfully to Judith's and Jael's in this aspect: all perceive the sexual, communal, life-giving, and death-dealing connections inherent in the sharing of food.

Esther's banquets resemble a combination of Jael's and Judith's, with this striking difference: through the process of requests and banquets in Esther, the enemy who is unbeknownst to himself endangered by the meal is split into two. Esther thus entertains two male guests: one powerful, drunk, and sexually interested, and the other the potential rapist whom the banquet dooms to die. Perhaps, in fact, she needs the second banquet to make the power of her pleasing reach through the two levels of influence—through the king to Haman.

The wine again rises to prominence here, referred to specifically three times, and always in reference to the king. Esther's request appears to be timed to coincide with the wine's effects on him, occurring "during the drinking of the wine" (7:2). The king is then so upset to hear her accusations against Haman (though she accuses Haman of actions that the king himself facilitated) that he leaves "the drinking of wine," then returns to "the banquet of wine" (7:8) to find Haman throwing himself at Esther's couch. Both time and position are, for the king, delineated in reference to his drinking. Although this is repeatedly referred to as a "banquet of wine," neither Esther nor Haman is said to feel the wine's effects. The point of the banquet, then, is to make the king's heart glad with wine; Esther has no need to please Haman similarly. Indeed, the very idea that Haman might be seeking pleasure from Esther is what finishes Haman off in the king's estimation. Ahasuerus responds to what he views as Haman's attempted rape by issuing his one direct order: that Haman be hanged (7:9).

While Jael and Judith sought to please the man in order to kill him, Esther seeks to please one man in order to kill another. Just as Esther has no need to intoxicate Haman, so she has no desire or need to kill the king. But she does need to destroy utterly this persona of the king, who wears his ring, plans to ride his horse, and seems about to sleep with his wife. Haman is in fact an aspect of the king's power; he is the king's egocentric pettiness turned against Mordecai the Jew, and against the Jews in general.

Haman's presence as the enemy aspect or agent of the king points out the story's efforts not to threaten the power structure, efforts that push the plot into a great fondness for indirection in general. Esther's delay in making her request thus needs to be seen in light of the text's general penchant for the mediated, delayed, and indirect. Intermediaries abound, as escorts, messengers, and advisors. The pronounced presence of writing in the story also relates to this indirection, as word goes out from the court through the mediation of the written text and its multiple translations. Other than the command to hang Haman, which is itself hinted at by the eunuch Harbona and of course by Esther, the king issues no direct commands but loans out his signet ring with alacrity. "The poor king," Charles Dorothy notes, "cannot seem to make a move throughout the Esther story without counsel."[12]

Perhaps most striking of the examples of indirection in the story is the fact that Esther must learn of the Jews' fate when word goes out from the court by means of a written edict and reaches Mordecai, whose reaction then boomerangs back by word of mouth to her (4:1–7). Outlining the placement of Esther and Mordecai in relation to the king, this particular indirect movement of information spotlights the results of Esther's "passing" and points to the relative functions of Esther and Mordecai in the story as a whole. Though Mordecai stands, as usual, outside the gates, he holds all the relevant information, including a copy of the edict itself and precise knowledge of the amount of money with which Haman bribed the king (4:7–8). Yet Esther, in her closeted space near to, but closed off from, the king himself, not only had not heard of the king's edict, but fails to understand

Mordecai's response to it.

Hearing that he is in sackcloth, she is "deeply distressed" (4:4), perhaps because she reads the sackcloth as indicative of poverty. Her gesture of sending him a new outfit resembles Marie Antoinette's suggestion that the peasants, lacking bread, ought to eat cake; in either case the woman of power interprets the symptoms of unrest superficially, and thus reveals her insular insensitivity. Charles Harvey notes that although she is terribly upset to hear that Mordecai is in sackcloth, Esther registers no reaction at all to hearing of the genocidal edict against the Jews.[13] But her verbal response to the delayed information and to Mordecai's request for her help shows that what she has lost in sensitivity to her own people, she has gained in knowledge of the court. "All the servants of the king and the people of his provinces," she tells him, know what Mordecai apparently does not, that no one may enter the king's presence uninvited (Est. 4:11). Mordecai knows in detail what the king proposes to do to the Jews. Esther was ignorant of this *what,* but she knows with great certainty *how* the power of the king operates, and how it is accessed, or not; of this how Mordecai's very position outside the city gates reveals his ignorance.

Just as the king and Haman can be read as two aspects of the royal powers that be, so Mordecai and Esther are two aspects of Jewish survival under that power: the male and the female. The male aspect seeks honor within the diaspora system and to some extent rules over the female, as Mordecai tells Esther what to do from Chapters 2–4. Mordecai is both the source and the endpoint of the action, since as father figure and first generation exile he represents Esther's roots, on the one hand, and the plot is resolved when he achieves his rightful place at court, on the other. He is the "what" of diaspora survival; he represents what ought to be honored by survival, what in fact ought to survive. Esther, on the other hand, is the "how." She has little contact with the Jewish traditions or people whom she is trying to preserve, but she is the means by which they are preserved. She is in this sense both more and less important than her cousin.

It is beneath Mordecai's dignity to bow before Haman, but not beneath Esther's to sleep with the king. Both the maintenance of dignity and its disregard are necessary to Jewish survival in this book, but the book is named for the one who let her own boundaries be crossed. The penetrated woman knows how to penetrate the boundaries of power—Esther, like Judith, by virtue of her beauty goes in where she ought to be forbidden, emerging with the prize of the enemy's death and the people's salvation.

REFLECTION QUESTIONS:

1. Can you identify a situation where you felt like an "other"?

2. If you were Vashti, what would you do differently to remain queen? How might Esther's importance be maintained in a different scenario?

3. Are there hidden rules in our society that makes a woman less "marriageable"?

4. Today, if one wines and dines and engages in intimacy with someone for a specific gain, they are negatively labeled. If there was an Esther situation today, would you agree or disagree with Esther's motives and actions?

5. Compare the roles of Mordecai and Esther in the saving of the Jews here. What is the contribution of each? How might each be a role model for activists today?

6. How far will you go to survive? Would you go to the length that Esther did for her people?

— FOUR —
HERODIAS

Banquet and Seduction in the Realm of Wrong

(READ MARK 6:14–29)

IF ESTHER'S WORLD IS LARGER and more complex than that of her narrative sisters, Herodias's world is narrower and less well lit. After a preamble that connects us rather loosely to the larger story of Mark's gospel, the story of John the Baptist's execution takes place entirely within the banquet hall or in direct relation to it. The time, too, though confused and displaced in relation to the gospel as a whole, is startlingly brief, both on the story and the discourse levels. That is, the story is told in a few verses, and within the story world, the action takes place entirely during the time of the banquet itself—the matter of a few hours, or even minutes, from beginning to end. The brevity of the story, like that of Jael's, increases its shock value for the reader. Though we know that John was beheaded before we hear how, John's severed head nevertheless makes its appearance suddenly, with too little ado and too steep a drop from the girl's pleasing dance to her gruesome request. The audience hardly has a chance to protest as Herod vacillates, before John's disciples are hauling his body away to its tomb.

In part, the abrupt feel of the story, again like that of Jael, is created by its several enigmas, primary among them being the question of what the story is doing here. The only passage in the gospels that does not star—or even feature—Jesus and his disciples, the story of John's execution suddenly confronts us with a new setting and characters, which have apparently only a slim connection to the setting and characters that we understood as those of the gospel. When Jesus sent his disciples off, we are told, Herod "heard" (6:14). What he heard is not clear, but apparently it had to do with Jesus, since it leads directly to a discussion of who Jesus might be. First, foremost, and finally comes the guess that Jesus is John the Baptist, revived. Others are guessing, in fact, but Herod seems quite certain, "The one whom I beheaded, John, that one has been raised" (v. 16).[1]

From this stark, haunted identification of both John and Jesus, we progress backwards somewhat awkwardly, toward a point where we can hear the story of how Herod beheaded John. Before Herod identified Jesus as John returned, we are told, Herod had had John arrested and put in prison. Before that, Herod had married his brother's wife, and after (or before?) the marriage, John had said that the union was illegal. After John said this (and after the marriage?), Herodias began to harbor a grudge against John, which explains why Herod put John in prison.

This state of affairs appears to have gone on for some time, since the verbs that describe it are entirely in the imperfect tense, reserved for actions continuous or repeated over a stretch of time.[2] From this point on (v. 20), time within the story begins to move forward again, and we return to the punctilear quality of aorist verbs, describing actions that occur one time in the past; thus we hear the story of the terrible birthday party. But the point at which time begins to move forward is not anchored in the time of the larger story.[3] With the dizzying backward movement of verses 14–19, we have lost the sense of when all of this took place in relation to the sending out of the disciples. By the time the story of John's execution actually begins, the reader is disoriented and may well wonder what he or she is doing here, in the nasty world of Herod's inner circle.

For that matter, the reader may wonder where "here" is. All we know about the place of John's execution is that Jesus is absent, and Herod is ruler. The gates of Herod's world are closed; only rumors of what Jesus has done can cross them, not Jesus himself. There are no miracles within this world, nor any hint of the coming realm of God; this may well be the only passage in the gospel that lacks both, excepting scenes from Jesus' own execution. In the place of the miraculous comes the altogether wrong.

Herod's marriage, first of all, is wrong. He has married his living brother's wife, an act that makes her an adulteress according to Jewish law. If Jewish law meant nothing for the book of Esther, it means a great deal for John, Herod, and Herodias in this story. John's one sentence here, "It is not lawful for you to have your brother's wife," implies that he sees Herod as a Jew expected to live according to the Torah.[4] The fact that Herodias is so stung by the criticism as to want John dead, and the fact that Herod imprisons John apparently for saying that the marriage is illegal, implies that they want to be seen as law-abiding Jews, and that they are Jewish enough to care what a prophet in the ancient tradition of prophets is saying.

But Herod's Jewishness, such as it is, conflicts with the title of "ruler" that the story gives him. Jewish rulers, in popular understanding at least, were born, not made. The gospels of Luke and Matthew understand Jewish kingship as remaining solely in David's line; hence their insistence that Jesus is descended from Davidic ancestry. Mark's lack of interest in such matters does not necessarily mean that he is ready to accept the Roman-supported and culturally Greek Herods as legitimate kings. In fact, Herod Antipas, the Herod who would have executed John the Baptist, did not even claim to be king, although his grandfather, Herod the Great, who ruled over more of what had been David's realm, had done so. Mark appears then to be granting kingship to the character of Herod simply for the purposes of this story. The question is why.

JEWS AND KINGS

Many readers of this passage have noted its resonance with the book of Esther, which we will address below, but fewer have seen the passage's place within a whole genre of stories from the Hebrew Bible and Jewish tradition, a genre to which Esther also belongs. The stories of Joseph and Daniel also feature wrongly imprisoned protagonists and an unreliable, manipulated ruler who more or less wants to do the right thing.[5] As Lawrence M. Wills describes them in his book, *Jew in the Court of the Foreign King*, these tales follow a pattern in which the wise diaspora Jew initially rises, then is opposed, put down, and endangered, and finally rises again, this time to new heights.[6]

As I have argued elsewhere, the story of John's execution resembles these court legends in interesting ways and differs from them in ways that are even more interesting.[7] Though initially John's virtues are praised by the king, John never rises to prominence on their account. Unlike Esther, he wins no one's favor; unlike Joseph, God does not cause whatever he touches to prosper (Gen. 39:23). Unlike Joseph as well, John is not imprisoned because of lies about his character; rather, Herod keeps John in prison knowing the truth about him, that he is "a righteous and holy man" (v. 20).

In the book of Daniel, King Darius, despite his admiration for Daniel, condemns him to the lions' den unwittingly, by means of a general decree that Daniel's enemies have orchestrated (Dan. 6:11–17). Similarly, Herod, despite his fear and admiration of John, is manipulated by John's enemies—using somewhat different methods—and unwittingly and unwillingly promises his way into John's execution. But Daniel emerges from the lions unscathed, causing Darius to praise the God of Israel; John, on the other hand, simply dies.

All of this assumes that John is in fact the main character at his own execution. But John hardly emerges as a character at all in this story. He is never fully on stage, but only heard as a voice, then dealt with as a corpse. Who the main character might be is an open question. The girl does more self-initiated acting than anyone else in the story, but this is a character who is, as Jean Delorme puts it, "without personal desire."[8] Empty of direction, the girl requires her mother, whose character consists of her one murderous intention, to supply her with a want, a need to be filled. The girl is a contentless form, while Herodias consists of the grudge, a pressing content that cannot be conveyed without the (bodily) form of the girl.

Whose story is this, anyway? No one seems to be doing what they intend to do. John is effectively bound and gagged, the girl has no intentions of her own, the mother has intentions she cannot carry out on her own, and Herod is committing acts he never intended. The main character here may well be John, since all the actions revolve around him, but his centrality is marked more by an absence than a presence. This story seems to achieve its effects generally in the negative. What makes John central is what he is not: free, active, powerful. Similarly, the meaning of the story emerges from what the story is not—an ultimately optimistic tale of Jewish survival under difficult circumstances.

Herodias's story in Mark 6 depends on stories that more closely fit Wills's definition of the court legend for its tension and horror. In those stories, the moral of the story seems to be that, though the foreign king is fickle and weak and the Jews' social position in the diaspora may be precarious, the virtuous and wise Jew will prevail to the benefit of all the Jews. With those stories as backdrop, the moral of this story becomes something much more pessimistic. There is no justice in this world, the king's weaknesses are fatal, and his vices inaccessible to the right kind of manipulation. The righteous and holy man is doomed. And all of this takes place not under a foreign king, though that is how the backdrop genre is defined, but under a king who is, as the story itself underlines, nominally Jewish.

Most likely, Mark calls Herod a king precisely for this reason. To see this story as related to those of the "Jew in the court of the foreign king" is to see Herod acting like a foreign king—foolish, corrupt, and easily manipulated. The reader does not expect a Persian or Babylonian to rule with the wisdom and piety of Israel's own ideal rulers. The diaspora stories rather hold out the hope that wise Jews may manage their affairs by managing the foolish foreigner in charge; these are stories of survival under the current state of affairs, not visions of an ideal state of affairs. But one ought not to have to manage a Jewish king. A Jewish king was the ideal; the court legends ought not to apply if the Jews are ruling themselves. The story of John's execution, by its framing as a court legend gone wrong, says that neither the ideal of sovereignty nor the manageable survival strategies of diaspora make sense with the world as it is.

CHARMING GIRLS AND EXECUTIONERS: ESTHER, HERODIAS, AND THE DAUGHTER

In a study that deals with both Esther and Herodias, comparison between the two proves as essential as it is inevitable.

Both stories involve royal banquets notable for the length of their guest lists; both women profit from promises a pleased ruler repeatedly makes to a charming girl. Both Herodias and Esther appear to be biding their time, awaiting the right opportunity to make their wishes come true. Like the similarities between Jael's and Esther's stories on the one hand and Judith's on the other, the similarities between Herodias and Esther emerge not simply from the commonalities of culture, but from some closer form of intertextuality, even reliance of the later text upon the earlier.

One of the more interesting connections between Esther and the Markan passage, particularly from a gender perspective, is the word used to describe each character. The word *kourasion*, translated "girl" and used here to describe Herodias's (nameless) daughter,[9] is also used in the Greek version of Esther to describe Esther herself and all the virgins gathered from the countryside. Like this girl, the girls in Esther strive to please the ruler. In their case, the virgins in Esther are compelled to be pleasing by the stakes of the contest, the outcome of which will greatly affect their life conditions. While Vashti refuses to come to a similar banquet even when summoned by the King, the girl in this story comes without escort or summons. Alice Bach notes this provision of entertainment at a men's gathering as "highly suspect." Wives and daughters would not have been present at such a celebration, Bach says, adding that, "The only women to be found at such gatherings were 'evil' women, ones who danced or entertained the men after the meal."[10] The girl's entry, then, and the fact that she is permitted to stay and entertain all and sundry does not speak well of the girl, her father, or the entire atmosphere at this court.

The manuscripts read awkwardly on the point of whose daughter this girl actually is—Herodias's, Herod's, or both.[11] If she is Herodias's daughter by her first marriage, there is a certain realism in the lascivious stepfather that Herod then becomes.[12] If she is Herod's daughter with Herodias, not only does the incestuous quality of whatever sexual attraction Herod shows increase dramatically, but the symmetry of the girl shuttling between her parents becomes still more intriguing. Yet the reader's confusion on this point may be relevant in itself. One wonders if, like the reader, Herod himself is confused as to whose daughter this is. Perhaps she is allowed to dance and entertain and is offered anything she wants precisely because Herod does not recognize her as Herodias's daughter, let alone his own, but sees her as an anonymous courtesan—which in a sense, she is.

While Judith and Esther manage to cross seemingly impenetrable boundaries by means of their beauty and charms, the daughter of Mark 6 does not even seem to notice that the boundaries exist. She enters the men's space blithely, neither taking note of any boundary nor being reminded of it by the men. But if the boundaries do not function to keep her out, they are quite effective for others. Though the center stage in this story is the banquet itself, two of its main characters—indeed the two characters whose conflict provides the story's drama—stand in the wings on either side of center.

Herodias, in particular, seems to be emphatically locked out. In order to mediate between her (step)father and mother, the girl must come in (v. 22), go out (v. 24), and come in again (v. 25), shuttling between the paternal seat of power and the maternal desires that have been exiled to power's margins. The social anxiety inherent in according free passage to female charms and sexuality becomes obvious here. What the ruler managed to keep at bay finds its way in with this girl and becomes real through the pleasures of the party.

The only other character who moves in and out of the banquet scene—this time in the other direction, toward

John—is the executioner. Herod "after sending an execution-er, commanded him to bring his head" (v. 26). Does Herod send for the executioner, or does he send someone already in his presence to become the executioner? The word translat-ed "executioner" appears only here in the New Testament; outside the New Testament it is more often an attendant or guard, someone who might occasionally be called upon to perform an execution. The word appears here in the accusa-tive case, the object of the participle "sending."

If, as the text seems to imply, an ordinary guard is sent from the banquet to the prison to return with John's head, then the movement of this guard *cum* executioner becomes a kind of counterpart to the movement of the girl. Indeed, not only are these the only two characters who cross the banquet's bound-aries, but they are the only two characters who move at all. Herod and his guests are at table, John in prison, and Herodias in her locked-out position throughout. Only these two agents of death, the one a conventional killer and the other in a sense an unconventional one, are able to move freely about the story. We might say that even the guard does not move freely, since he does only and exactly as he is told to do—he goes away; he comes back with the head.

But then, Herod also is doing only what he is told to do, and so, in a sense, is the girl. When the guard returns with John's head, the verbs proliferate without a stated subject so that it is possible to become confused as to whether Herod himself or the guard is doing the action. "And going away, he beheaded him in the prison. And he brought his head on a platter"—up to this point the pronouns presumably refer to the guard, but the next is questionable: "and he gave it to the girl" (vv. 27–28). The guard gave it to the girl? Or Herod gave it to the girl? The girl, after all, did not ask the guard for it; she asked Herod. If in fact we read the subject of "gave" as Herod, then we are forced to wonder how long Herod has been the subject. Who brought the head on a platter? Who performed the execution? This last question, which may seem absurd, finds support beforehand in Herod's introductory pronouncement, concerning "John, whom I myself beheaded." The pronoun *ego*, "I", unnecessary in the Greek, adds emphasis on Herod as the beheader. If Herod's hand did not wield the ax, the anonymous executioner is nevertheless terribly close to being identified with him. But the executioner can go, bring, come back, while Herod is stuck, in several senses.

The girl's movement becomes all the more striking since she goes to and fro of her own volition—coming in without being summoned, going out on her own accord, and returning with an apparent enthusiasm for the message from her mother. All this, and she dances too. This initial movement for movement's sake becomes all the more enthralling since everyone else in the story seems unable to move at all. No wonder Herod is so greatly entertained. Stuck in this world himself, he is bemused by John's word from elsewhere and enthralled by the girl's bodily freedom, which seems likewise to come from without.

There is a moment in Esther, as Mordecai informs her of the edict against the Jews, when we wonder whether Esther's loyalty is with her people or not, whether her passing has completely elided what it hides. Then Esther comes through and the reader is reassured; because Esther really is a Jew, the Jews will survive and the story continues. In Esther, the girl who charms the ruler is good, and her loyalties are to her cousin and the Jewish people. By stark contrast the charming girl in Mark 6 is of dubious moral character and intention, and her loyalties are to a technically adulterous mother, outlawed by the Jewish people. If Herodias's daughter is also Herod's daughter, then the very existence of the girl is illegal, excluded by Jewish law along with the adultery that created her.

While Esther through her own beauty and ability to please manipulates Ahasuerus, Herodias must use her daughter's pleasing qualities to manipulate Herod. Bach notes that if we put gender concerns aside, "the character of Herodias would have no parallel in the Esther story."[13] In comparing the Esther story to this one, Esther's character resides somewhere between that of Herodias and the daughter. Herodias resembles Esther in her desire to manipulate the ruler to an execution but differs from her in both her methods and her aims.

Herodias needs her daughter as accomplice. In Esther, the ruler's power to do the Jews good and his power to do them harm were divided between Ahasuerus and Haman. Here the charming girl and the angry, plotting woman are similarly divided into two. The adult woman with the agenda is hidden and unfed, while her daughter travels freely into forbidden places and uses the powers of her dance to gain not her own but her mother's desires "on a platter." In fact, the girl may be adding the detail of the platter because in the context of the banquet and her mother's absence, the request strikes her as motivated by hunger.

The relationship between the mother and daughter is perhaps the most troubling of those in the story. The question for Bach and other readers is whether the girl is an innocent child, or whether she is actively seducing Herod. The girl's dance, though it looms large in the art inspired by this story, is described briefly in the text: "And when the daughter of Herodias went in and danced, she pleased the ruler and the guests" (v. 22a). The act of dancing itself resides only in one unmodified participle. Furthermore, in part because the sense of time is so surreal in this story, we have no sense of the girl's age. Mark uses the same word, *kourasion,* to describe the girl of twelve whom Jesus raises from the dead (5:41–42), whom Jesus also refers to as a child (5:39).

A twelve-year-old girl might be either seductive (given the wrong sort of upbringing) or entirely naïve, or both. This girl, furthermore, could be anywhere from four years old to the upper limits of unmarried girls, perhaps fifteen or so. It is the ruler's response, overabundant as it is, as well as our society's tendency to project all sexuality onto the female, that leads us to imagine a belly dancer skilled in the art of seduction. Bach concludes on the contrary that the girl is simply a tool of her mother. "The biblical account of the dance is innocent, a child charming an adult audience . . . the female power belongs to Herodias, who controls the movements of her daughter."[14] But in a sense it hardly matters. The lack of a strong desire to kill does not necessarily mean the girl is wholly innocent. Certainly Herod's lack of enthusiasm for John's death does not exonerate him from guilt. Whether the girl wills it or not, she is, like Herod, the executioner, and even the guests, a cog in the machine that produces John's death. No one is good or innocent here, except the one who is dead.

In the other stories we have looked at, the death that is the story's aim is to some extent justified through the course of the meal. In this story, however, the killing is not justified at all, but the wrongful death of a righteous man. Jael's story does not concern itself with justifying the murder of Israel's enemy and so does not include food that would remind the reader that killing is necessary. Her story offers little justification because justification does not seem to be required. But in the case of Herodias, no justification is offered because none will suffice.

Ironically, the kill-to-eat motif absent in Judges 4–5 emerges here, obscenely, as John's head appearing at the banquet on a platter suggests that it constitutes dessert. Unfortunately, it feeds the wrong people. Judith takes Holofernes's head in her food sack back to the elders of

Bethulia, and it strengthens and sustains them like the food they have been lacking. John's head may also sustain Herodias and/or the guests at Herod's party, but that is not good news. The entire tale of a woman getting the better of a man by seduction, by satiating him one way or another, is turned on its severed head in Mark 6. The reader who knows and loves Esther and Judith hates Herodias, the more so for her resemblance to them.

PATTERNS OF PLEASURE AND POWER

Herodias has only one speech in the story, and it appears to be something she has been holding in her mouth with the grudge against John but has been powerless to voice until now. Her daughter's question, "What shall I ask for?" allows Herodias to speak for the first and only time, so that her murderous desire, "the head of John the Baptizer," moves outward from her, through the girl, inexorably through the chain of power until it becomes real in the severed head.

Once the words are out of Herodias's mouth, there is no stopping them. The girl, for her part, seems downright happy to convey the request to her father. She returns to the banquet "immediately, with haste" and requests that the head be given to her "at once" and "on a platter" (v. 25). The addition of the platter may be an expression of squeamishness; perhaps she does not want to touch it. But given her lack of hesitation in conveying the request, the platter more likely marks the girl as affirming and signing on to her mother's request, making it her own. Rene Girard wonders, in fact, if the girl is not taking her mother's request all too literally. "In Greek, as in English, to demand someone's head is to demand his death. Period." The girl, not getting the part-for-the-whole metaphor in her mother's request, understands her mother as literally wanting John's head, and consequently adds the practical detail of the platter.[15]

As Delorme notes, the platter also works for purposes of display, rather like posting the head on a spike.[16] But perhaps most strikingly, it is the head's position on a platter that makes it into the final course at this banquet. Thus the girl, who enters and is welcomed at the meal, catalyzes and frames the substance of it by causing John's head to be presented as food, the only food we see at this banquet.

On the other side of the stage, John waits in prison. Though Herod recognizes John's virtue and holiness, he has been keeping it under lock and key. A prisoner of the court and not a member of it, John is not present at the banquet and, as far as the story tells us, has been silenced with his imprisonment. He exists in prison but does not speak. Like Herodias, he lacks the power to speak, and also like her he has only one line in this story. But while he has spoken once before being silenced, Herodias lives in silence until she can speak through the mouth of her daughter. At the opening of the banquet, both Herodias and John are silent, unable to speak to power. But while John's speech to Herod has already failed to get rid of Herodias, Herodias's speech will not fail to get rid of John. In and of themselves, the male words of the law are impotent, imprisoned. But a woman's words voiced by a girl's body are free to go anywhere, and they wield the power of life and death.

Delorme makes an interpretive link between the two mentions of Herod's pleasure: First he "gladly" listens to John; then he "is pleased" watching the daughter's dance.[17] These are presumably two different kinds of pleasure. And even if the daughter's dance is not particularly sexual, there seems to be little contest between the two pleasures for Herod. He keeps John alive for the sake of the odd, perplexed pleasure that John's words provide him; but for the pleasure with which the girl provides him, he is willing to give anything, even up to half of his realm—even, as it turns out, the life of those perplexing, pleasant words.

As we saw earlier, the condition in which we find these characters at the start of the party has apparently been going on for some time. The imperfect verbs of verses eighteen through twenty indicate that it has been Herodias hating John and Herod listening to him gladly for a time made longer by its inherent tension. John stands poised on the brink of execution with the force of Herodias's will unable to push him over, but nevertheless making its ominous presence known. He is hanging on by the thread of his words and their effect on Herod. The function of the girl is to cut that thread. When Herod turns toward the immediate pleasures of the girl's dance, he is unconsciously turning away from whatever pleasure John's words afforded him, and this is Herodias's intent, if not the girl's. The silent dance proves louder than John's words and silences finally the lone criticism that Herod could hear.

The girl accomplishes this resolution fittingly, since if she is Herod's daughter, then she is in fact the product of their illegal marriage. In her we see embodied the union of female desire to kill with the male power to kill. As she shuttles between the two, she brings them together, facilitating the reaction in the definition of a catalyst, exposing and producing the hidden potentials of both. No one person in this story has both the will and the power to kill. Will and power are vested in different people, and the girl—who in a sense has neither—unites them.

In this story, as the artistic renderings in theatre and paint rarely fail to point out, everyone is in a tension-fraught relationship to everyone else. We have discussed the power triangle (not a love triangle, as some of the theatrical versions would have it) of Herod, John, and the girl, as well as the opposition between the offstage characters of Herodias and John, and the all-too-close relationship of mother and daughter. But the triangular relationship of Herodias to John and Herod also makes itself felt.

In Esther, we saw that the masculine powers that be were split into two, one who must be pleased, and one who must die. Jewish survival was threatened by Haman, who is an aspect of the king's power, a manifestation of his power to kill. Like Esther, Herodias uses one man's pleasure to kill another man. But Haman and John, otherwise, contrast so drastically as to make comparison almost impossible. Haman's initial position in relation to the ruler is grand—all the populace (but one) bows before Haman, who dines with the ruler, makes laws for the ruler—is in fact, one with the ruler, until Esther steps in. John, on the other hand, has no power and only the most strained intimacy with the ruler. The epitome of powerlessness, he is in one sense in prison from the beginning of this passage—in another sense he is already dead. In fact, the convoluted way in which the first few verses of this story progress leaves the impression that John has always been in prison, even when he was preaching against Herod's marriage and even when Herod was listening to him gladly. Certainly, unlike Haman, John never eats with the King. Indeed, John's eating habits would not be conducive to a banquet in fine society, or any society. Last we heard, John was eating the locusts and wild honey he found in the wilderness, shunning human culture along with the evils of human society (Mark 1:6). When we hear the story of this banquet, it suddenly seems that John's aversion to society was justified. Better locusts and honey, after all, than human body parts.

What Herodias manages to kill, then, may be an aspect of the king, but it is an aspect that the king himself has locked away. Rather than the hand that wields the king's destructive power, John is an occasional, disembodied voice in the king's head—interesting, disturbing even, but impotent even while he is alive. This voice Herodias wants to silence, not because it threatens to destroy her—as Haman did Esther—but because it judges her. John's criticism is a one-line voice from outside this backwater world where everything is wrong, where men are entertained by the bodies of their own daughters, and where adultery rules.

As long as King Herod rules here, the bizarre is the status quo and no longer bizarre. But John's imprisoned voice points out that it is in fact bizarre, unlawful, wrong. What John says is not even particularly harsh. He does not call Herodias a whore or even accuse the couple directly of adultery. He simply states the fact that their marriage is not legal; it is not proper, appropriate, normal. But precisely because Herod is ready to listen to John's voice defining normalcy, Herodias wants that voice silenced. If standards other than those she and Herod make themselves are to be applied to them, then Herodias will emerge indeed an adulteress, something that needs to be cast off in order to make things right. By law, the punishment for an adulterous woman was stoning. As difficult as it is to feel sorry for the evil Herodias of this passage, the fact remains that Herod can afford to listen gladly to John—he has much less to lose.

While Jael's story at once celebrates and fears the hidden killing potential of women, Herodias's does not celebrate, but only abhors and fears a killing power hidden in the very impotence of the woman's social position. Herodias longs to kill, but unlike Jael, she cannot do so herself. Neither does she face a singular enemy, as did Jael and Judith, but finds herself up against an entire world of men influencing other men. This is a fractured world—both male and female representations of power are split and appear in two or more manifestations. Movement and action are constricted for all but the

dancing girl, and the other characters' restrictions are almost
as severe as those of the bound and imprisoned John. Neither
the woman killer nor the man to be killed can act directly, or
at all. In Judges 4 and in Judith, the man and woman faced off
in a tent, where the woman killed the man with her own
hands, albeit in Judith's case with his weapon in her hands.

In this story, by contrast, the movement from Herodias to
John—separated by the banquet from which both are
exiled—has to pass through the daughter, the ruler, his guests,
and his executioner before Herodias can, like Judith, hold the
man's head in her hand.

A final note of comparison between this story and the others we have looked at: Although the action here takes place
at a banquet, no one seems to be eating. As opposed to the
incessant mentions of wine in Esther and the distinctions
made in Judith between the kosher food and wine and that
of Holofernes, here a great many important people have
gathered for a banquet at which there is, in the text at least,
neither food nor wine. Granted, Herod acts as though he is
drunk. He is pleased by the girl, like the tipsy Ahasuerus is
pleased with Esther, and like Ahasuerus as well, Herod speaks
repeatedly. He speaks without forethought or insight, without realizing the implications of what he is saying and without really knowing to whom he is saying it.

In Esther, much of this was attributed to the effects of the
wine—though the wine seemed to affect only the ruler.
Here, however, we are never told that Herod is drunk or even
that there is wine at the party. Rather, the girl herself seems
to put Herod under the influence. Judith used her beauty and
charms together with a great deal of alcohol to get
Holofernes where she wanted him, but this girl uses only her
dance to do so. Herod is perhaps left without Holofernes's
reasonable excuses; Herod was not drunk, only stupid. If the
girl makes Herod drunk, she also provides the food. John's

head, arranged on a platter, becomes the only food we hear about at this important and crowded party. And indeed, the guests at this feast will not be satisfied until they get that precise dish, or so Herod thinks (v. 26). So at this men's banquet, from which women are supposed to be excluded, a girl slips in, and with her a woman's will. Together they provide the men with the very substance of their party—entertainment, drunkenness, and food.

REFLECTION QUESTIONS:

1. In some settings, do you feel inhibited to express your Christianity for fear of being criticized or thought of as a religious fanatic?

2. What fuels Herodias's desire to have the head of John the Baptist? Might it have been more than what he said about her marriage to Herod?

3. Why does Herodias need her daughter as an accomplice?

4. Do you think Herod would have honored the request for John's head had Herodias asked for it rather than her daughter?

5. If the moral of the court legends (Joseph, Daniel, Esther) is that the virtuous Jew can manage to thrive in the diaspora, what would the moral of the story of John's execution be?

6. What does the story of John's execution have to do with the larger story of Mark's gospel?

— FIVE —

ABIGAIL

Murder, Shalom, and the Lack Thereof

(READ 1 SAMUEL AND 2 SAMUEL)

READERS MAY WONDER what the rather virtuous and bloodless tale of Abigail and David has to do with the treacherous waters of murder and manipulation in which we have been swimming. Abigail never comes near a bed in her story, nor does she involve herself in a killing. Yet like Jael, Judith, Esther, and Herodias, Abigail uses a context of feeding to please and manipulate a man with power, and like them, she benefits from a man in power's death. True, Abigail is not a killer. She does not pick up her own weapon as did Jael, nor the man's weapon as does Judith, nor even the man himself, as Esther and Herodias do, to kill. On the contrary, rather than using David to kill, she prevents him from killing. But that is not necessarily to say that Abigail does not want Nabal dead. Though she does not explicitly express such a desire, she does fail to contradict or reprimand the servant who calls Nabal a "son of wickedness," and herself dismisses Nabal to David as a useless, harmful fool. More importantly, she appears ready and willing to benefit from Nabal's death once it is accomplished.

Indeed, despite the lack of any stated desire to kill, despite her intervention that prevents David from killing, despite the fact that Nabal dies explicitly and directly at God's hand,

Abigail often is blamed for her husband's death. David Jobling reads Abigail as a kind of unseen (more so than God, apparently) hand behind the killing.

> That Abigail has murderous feelings toward Nabal fits into the pattern of their relationship as the story has built it up, from the contrastive introduction of the two characters (v. 3) through Abigail's intriguing with the servants behind Nabal's back (vv. 14–19) to her insulting him before David (v. 25). It agrees above all with her wish that David's enemies might be like Nabal, which can only mean a wish that Nabal might be dead. (v. 26)[1]

In Jobling's reading, the story subtly portrays Abigail as "desiring and working for the death of the husband who stands in the way of the desired marriage."[2]

This reading is based in part on the assumption that Abigail loves David and wants nothing more than to be his wife, an assumption that I will question below. But before we delve into the evidence from which Jobling draws his conclusion, let us state the obvious. Abigail, far from being an accessory to murder here, is the agent of peace. She certainly despises Nabal—who doesn't? We are told that he is bad and she is good, in exactly those terms (v. 3). Her lack of respect for him may be a breach of traditional marital codes, but it also shows her good sense. In fact, it is not Abigail whom we see "desiring and working for the death of the husband," but David.

Yet the temptation to read more motives than we are told into the story is almost impossible to resist. The story is rife with what might have been: disaster, bloodbath, and endless consequent guilt averted. Abigail barely manages to prevent David from a mass killing and from incurring bloodguilt; on this would-have-been disaster the story hinges. David, with his men, both prevented and refrained from destroying, steal-

ing, or killing when they guarded Nabal's flocks and shepherds in the wilderness. Barbara Green notes that it is this
lack of event for which David seems to want recompense
from Nabal.[3] The fact that nothing happened to the shepherds in the wilderness, nothing was stolen from them, none
of them were mistreated—this absence of destruction is what
David gave Nabal, in exchange for the food that David now
requests. This act of refraining from or preventing harm is
referred to no less than three times in the story—first by
David in his message to Nabal (v. 7), then by Nabal's servant
in his report to Abigail (v. 15), and then again as David moves
towards the slaughter he plans when he appears to be simply
muttering to himself, rehearsing the grievance that drives
him to kill (v. 21). The weight of what might have happened—the shepherds might have been hurt, their sheep or
belongings might have been stolen, David might have killed
every male in the household—presses on the story, in which
very little actually does happen.

In what we might call the story proper, all that occurs is a
great deal of conversation—David's young men speak to
Nabal and he to them, then they report back to David.
Meanwhile, one of Nabal's servants goes to Abigail, begging
her to do something. In response to the two reports of
Nabal's insult, David approaches Nabal's household with
killing in mind, and Abigail approaches David with preventing killing in mind. They meet and talk. Then Abigail goes
home in peace and David goes back where he came from,
and that really ought to be that. Thus far in the story, the central event is one that did not occur—David did not kill every
male in Nabal's household. But in the epilogue, much more
dramatic events take place. Here Nabal dies at God's hand,
and David marries Abigail, or more literally, "he took her as
a woman/wife" (v. 42). In the first thirty-five verses of the
story, nothing fundamentally changes in the characters' lives

or relationships; then in the last four verses, there is a complete, abrupt, and hurried reshuffling of loyalties, lives, and property. What happens to mark the division is divine intervention. If anyone has the right to kill, to take one man's wife and give her to another man, it is God.

Curiously similar to the Herodias interlude, the story of Abigail meeting David, including its epilogue, seems to be sandwiched between pieces of a larger, ongoing tale. Green reads the story as a "sideshadow," an episode that "branches off to sketch laterally what might have but did not take place"; that is, to reframe with different characters and setting a piece of the larger story, and to imagine it turning out differently.[4] Like many critics, Green sees this chapter primarily in relation to the chapters before and after, both of which are accounts of Saul's pursuing David. She and others point out that in Chapter 25 we see David arming himself to slaughter the household of a man who resembles Saul in several ways. Yet here as in Chapters 24 and 26, David ultimately refrains from killing and lets God deal with the problem. That is, Chapter 25 seems to be less a way of rewriting the story of Saul with a different ending than it is a repetition of the theme of Chapters 24 and 26—that David had every right to behave much more violently than he actually did. In these stories we see David as possessing the power to kill, yet thus far we can still maintain our image of him as a man of peace.

On another level, though, David's commitment to the *shalom* he initially heaps upon Nabal is shallow and short-lived. "Go up to Carmel and go to Nabal and greet him in my name for *shalom*," David tells his young men, "and say this: '*Shalom* to you and *shalom* to your household and *shalom* to all that is yours'" (vv. 5–6). Most translators render *shalom* as "peace," though Jon D. Levenson prefers "prosperity."[5] Marjorie O'Rourke Boyle agrees that the Hebrew word has legal and financial connotations, its root meaning being "payment" or "retribution."[6] Levenson notes: "It is precisely Nabal's attitude toward his holdings which destroys the potential for the *shalom* with David which the latter seeks."[7] Others question whether David is in fact seeking shalom. Green notes that the shift in David's tone from addressing Nabal as "your son, David," to strapping on his sword is abrupt and dramatic.[8] If David was seeking shalom, it was a shalom entirely on his own terms, and short of those terms, he is ready to personally take shalom, whether translated as "peace" or "prosperity," from Nabal's household.

The return to peace, or rather the diversion of the action from the road to violence, is entirely up to Abigail. Her response to the threat David poses to her and to her servants is food. She hurries out to meet David with a generous gift of supplies for his men. So as he comes toward Nabal intent on killing, she goes from Nabal to him, intent on feeding. In this sense and in others, this is an encounter fraught with issues of life and death. David wants to live. The hospitality codes are built on the premise that travelers in the wilderness depend for their survival on the generosity of hosts along the way. Nabal has refused to display that generosity, and consequently doomed David and his men to hunger, thirst, and possibly to death, while Nabal himself feasts and drinks. But David wants to live, and he is willing, even eager, to kill all the males in Nabal's household—and most likely to eat some of them, assuming that male animals are also included[9]—in order that he and his men may live. Abigail's intercession makes this unnecessary—with her gift of food and her soothing of David's wounded dignity, it becomes possible for David to survive, physically and socially, without killing Nabal. Once she has given the food and the words, and he has received both, David is ready to again send shalom in Nabal's general direction, telling Abigail, "Go in shalom to your home."

MEN AND A WOMAN, LOVE AND FEAR

Abigail's success in reviving shalom relates directly to her gender. Caught between David and his young men on the one hand and Nabal and his (male) servants on the other, Abigail appears to be the only woman in the country. When Nabal throws down the gauntlet to David, and David takes it up with alacrity, everyone except Nabal sees disaster as imma-nent for Nabal and his household. David vows in his mutter-ing to kill every male belonging to Nabal, and Nabal's servant seems convinced that he can. Abigail's rush to placate David and her obsequiousness in doing so exhibits her belief that the servant is right: The situation is urgent and dire.

Nabal's servant himself, seeing slaughter on the horizon, seems powerless to do anything about it. His pleading with Abigail lacks any specific request for what she ought to do; nevertheless, he clearly wants her to act. In large part he talks to Abigail simply because no one can talk to Nabal. The mes-sage that the servant brings to Abigail—in effect, "we are all about to die; do something!"—bears a striking resemblance to that which Mordecai sends to Esther. Like Esther, Abigail seems to have been unaware of the events that now require her action. Abigail herself later tells David, "I your servant did not see my master's men whom you sent!" (v. 26). Like Esther as well, Abigail's position as wife of the man in power puts her in a unique position to neutralize that man's mistakes. In both cases, the fact that the one who must act is a woman has both kept her ignorant of the impending crisis and given her options for dealing with it that other characters do not have.

Like Judith, Jael, and in a sense like Esther as well, Abigail goes out from her home to meet the man she must please, crossing boundaries that others would or do find treacherous. Nabal has effectively put distance between himself and

David. Though David's men "were a wall" surrounding and protecting the shepherds in Nabal's fields (v. 16), Nabal does his best to erect a wall to keep them out. The story sets up two alternative ways to cross this distance, the distance implied in Nabal's rhetorical questions to the effect that he does not know the son of Jesse. This is a distance, then, composed of ignorance as well as animosity.

First David sets out to cross this intervening territory with swords and men as his passport. Then, in answer, Abigail sets out in the opposite direction, with food to assure her safe passage. Abigail, like Judith, packs up her food and sets off from her own camp to that of her enemy, the man who attacks her people. There is even in both stories a ravine to symbolize the boundary, the gap that must be bridged between the two. Like Judith, Abigail is beautiful and wise, but for Abigail neither wisdom nor beauty acts as her password to assure her safe travel across the borderlands.

Abigail's safe passage seems to depend entirely on the food. Her gender sets her up as nurturer and feeder. As the only woman in Nabal's household, the only woman David's men encounter, she appears to be the only person equipped either to feed them or to peacefully cross the distance that Nabal has established. David's way across the divide set up by these two groups of men, these two leaders, is a man's way, made for men. Abigail's way is one traveled only by the food and the story's only female, herself.

Nabal's servant tells Abigail that disaster looms on the whole household, but David's oath targets only the males. All males or, as the King James literally translates the Hebrew idiom, "everything that pisseth against the wall," must stand in for their master and die for Nabal's rudeness. Strictly speaking, then, Abigail's own life is not in danger. Indeed, hers may be the only life not in danger, since she is the only female mentioned in the passage. David's young men are wandering warriors, who have presumably left any female family members behind them. Nabal likewise is surrounded by shepherds and shearers, all male as far as we know. The use of idioms like "put on each man his sword," and Nabal's "many servants are breaking away, each man from his master" underlines the masculinity of these groups, as does David's oath itself. As a woman, Abigail has, in a sense, no business in this quarrel.

Yet the reader instinctively, or perhaps from having read other biblical narratives, knows that a battle between men will affect any woman who may be nearby. When Simeon and Levi take revenge for their sister's rape, they target the males just as David does, debilitating and then killing them. But when the men and boys are dead, the other brothers join in to destroy what remains and to seize the women and children as loot (Gen. 34:27–29). Rape is involved, implied, and approved in that brief description; it is an understood privilege of the victors that, having killed the adult men, they may take ownership of the surviving women through rape. Abigail's future as the wife of a conquered, murdered man is thus not bright. Since what David was after originally was a guest's share of Nabal's property, it seems likely that killing all the males is in part aimed to liberate all that belonged to them, including their wives and daughters. Abigail is likely to be raped, and to fall from the position of a wealthy man's wife to that of a slave or concubine.

Like Jael, then, Abigail goes out to greet a man who may be coming to rape her, among his other aims. Yet she seems to bear her potential rapist no ill will. Like Jael, she welcomes him, feeds him, flatters him, but unlike Jael, Abigail never turns against him. If she can prevent him from killing her husband and raping her, then the husband's death and her use as sexual object can occur legitimately, in which case, given David's immanent ascension to the throne, her position has risen rather than fallen. Like Tamar, who will be raped by Abigail's own son in Second Samuel, Abigail tries (in her case successfully) to talk her would-be rapist into taking possession of her by peaceful, socially acceptable means, means that will not shame her or her household (2 Sam. 13:13).

LET HIM EAT WORDS

While Abigail's gift of food carries symbolic weight as a kind of transference of life from Nabal to David, David in fact never is said to eat the food. The banquet in this story is not the food served by Abigail, but the meal at which Nabal appears to be both host and solitary guest, honoring himself like the king that David will be. Fittingly, Abigail gives Nabal's food to David—or rather, the food that should be eaten by Nabal's men ("for my shearers"[v. 11]) to David's men ("let the gift . . . be given to the men who follow at the feet of my master"[v. 27]). But Abigail and David do not share a meal; the meal that the gift of food will be is not consummated, as the hints of a sexual relationship remain hints. Neither, though, does Abigail share food or drink with her husband, whom she has left to his own pleasures while she corrects his mistakes. The meal with which Abigail provides David is all content with no form—the food and the conversation being emphatic and abundant, but there being no reclining, at table or otherwise. On the other hand, the meal that Nabal indulges in is all form with no content—a banquet fit for a king, with no guests, no food to speak of, and no words.

Clearly, food is key in understanding the story's relationships. The story begins amid Nabal's "three thousand sheep and a thousand goats" (v. 2). Nabal has an abundance of pastoral wealth, and his wealth takes the form of walking food. David appeals to Nabal for "whatever your hand finds," implying that food is always within Nabal's easy grasp, and his request is bolstered by the fact that this is "a good day" (v. 8). The reference is to the sheep-shearing David has already mentioned—the time for shearing was a time of feasting, when gifts of food to those with less would have been expected. Nabal, however, draws a line around those he will feed and those he will not. "Now should I take my bread and my water and the meat I have slaughtered for my shearers and give it to unknown men from who knows where?" (v. 11). He implies that this is a zero sum game; if the meat goes to David's men, it will not go to the shearers for whom it was intended. His own servant's errand to Abigail a few minutes later, however, implies that Nabal's concern for and solidarity with the shearers and shepherds is not as he presents it. In fact, if this servant is any example, Nabal's men want to be commensal with David's men—the two parallel groups would like to merge in the act of eating. Only Nabal stands between them. His banquet then becomes an emblem of anticommensality. Rather than join his own with David's in the meal David requests, Nabal eats alone, while a battle motivated by hunger brews around him.

Abigail's food then needs to be generous in order to neutralize this explosive situation. Indeed, the food she takes with her is by far the most detailed description of food that we read in any of these five stories: "Abigail hurried and took two hundred loaves of bread and two skins of wine and five dressed sheep, and five seahs of roasted grain and a hundred raisin cakes and two hundred pressed figs and she loaded it onto the donkeys" (v. 18). Yet Abigail's gift of food appears merely window dressing beside her generous display of verbiage.

What returns the word shalom to David's mouth is not in fact Abigail's food, but her words, which seem to take on a life of their own. Her speech is convoluted—perhaps in an effort to befuddle David and thus divert him from his purpose.[10] Levenson finds the entire exchange between Abigail and David "touching," which seems to imply that he takes Abigail at her word in her subservience. To my ear, her speech is a combination of prophecy that seems to spring up out of nowhere and the most obvious kind of flattery, all designed to save herself, her household, and even her worthless husband.

Rather than simply beginning to speak, her speech self-consciously announces itself: "Let your servant now speak into your ears and hear the words of your servant" (v. 24). She initially takes the blame onto herself, but apparently only so that she can be accepted as spokesperson and negotiator for the household. She does not seem inclined to be blamed, much less punished, for Nabal's mistake. Rather, although she appears to be trying to save his life, among others, she distances herself from Nabal's insulting behavior, telling David to disregard "the heart of this man of wickedness Nabal," and that "I your servant did not see the men of my master whom you sent" (v. 25). Essentially, she is asking David to hear her words instead of Nabal's, and asking him, in disregarding Nabal's heart, to disregard his foolish words as well. In the very next sentence, she is speaking as though David's restraint were already accomplished: "since the Lord has kept you from coming to bloodshed and from avenging yourself with your own hand" (v. 26), she says. Then she presents the food to David's men, this time asking for forgiveness (rather than disregard) for Nabal, and somehow basing her request on just how great God is going to make David and his kingship. He will have a great house and win many battles and when God appoints him as ruler over Israel, then he certainly does not want to have any "staggering or stumbling of the heart of my master, that he shed blood needlessly or avenged my master, and now may your enemies and the ones intending to harm my master be like Nabal" (v. 26). Jobling, as quoted above, understands this as a kind of prolepsis, that Abigail is speaking of Nabal as though he were already dead, which he very soon will be. Indeed, it is hard to imagine, as Jobling points out, that Abigail wishes that all David's enemies be as Nabal is at that moment—eating and drinking himself into a stupor. And there is certainly a foreshadowing, at the least, of Nabal's death in this grim line: Abigail's foreknowledge of David's future leadership makes a prediction of Nabal's death sound reasonable. Yet Abigail has said that Nabal was a worthless, wicked fool—one to be disregarded utterly. Could she be wishing that all David's enemies were so easily ignored? The other possibility, a reading that might even accompany one or more of these, is that Abigail's emphasis is that David's enemies should be like Nabal, and David himself should not be.

Nabal is, after all, according to his servant, a man who cannot be reasoned with, who cannot be spoken with—exactly as Abigail is trying to reason with David. In fact, Nabal seems to be characterized by a lack of conversation. After he rebukes David's men, the servant proclaims to Abigail that no one can speak to Nabal, and then Abigail, in apparent agreement, pointedly avoids speaking to Nabal both before and after going to speak to David. Beforehand, she does not tell him what she is about to do (v. 19b). Afterwards, she does not speak to him at all until the next morning, and when she does, the results are ultimately fatal (vv. 36–38). Nabal does not do well with conversations; few will try to talk with him, and he reacts badly to those who do. The question then becomes, how will David react? Is David a man who can be talked to or not? For the moment, it seems, David is indeed a man to whom one can talk. Certainly Abigail does talk to him, at some length. When she is finished, after David praises God and Abigail and sends her on her way in peace, he himself points out what a reasonable man he is: "See," he tells her, "I have heard your voice" (v. 36). Her voice, and David's hearing of it, has kept him from killing. Likewise her voice, her words, will stop Nabal's heart, facilitating the killing to be done by God.

THE WAY TO A MAN'S HEART

How we are to understand Nabal's stony paralysis and subsequent death remains an open question. Boyle persuasively demonstrates that there is no biblical Hebrew equivalent for the English word "petrified," with its double meaning of "turned to stone" and "terrified."[11] She also points out what perhaps ought to be obvious: that Israelite medical science did not understand the circulatory system, nor did it view pumping blood to the body as the heart's physical function. Hence the story cannot be telling us that Nabal had a heart attack, however much that interpretation may suggest itself to the modern reader. The word *lev,* translated heart, might have in fact a broader meaning, more like the colloquial "guts." Nabal died inside, it appears, and turned to stone. Boyle argues that in doing so, Nabal fully becomes what he has been inherently all along, since words meaning "wither, fade, die," and "carcass, corpse" are derived from the same root as this fool's unlikely name.[12]

But why should Abigail's report kill Nabal's insides? Is he despondent at his wife's and servants' betrayal? Boyle believes that the stoniness is not despondency at all, but simply Nabal moving further down the road of obstinacy and hard-headed /hard-heartedness that he has been on all along. Nabal hears about David's conversation with his wife and becomes even more stubborn and pig-headed.[13] Yet if Boyle is right, we might expect Nabal to do something with his stubborn animosity. But instead, his turning to stone seems to lead inexorably to his death at God's hand ten days later. Having turned to stone seems to make him an easier target for Yahweh's wrath.

If Nabal's reaction is neither terror nor recalcitrance, then in what sense did his heart die inside him? We may need to push the question back to the report that seems to cause Nabal's inner death. Abigail comes back to her husband after meeting David for the first time and having prophesied to David that he will be king. She finds Nabal, that son of Belial, holding a banquet for himself "like the banquet of a king" (v. 36). Green reads Nabal as in "splendid isolation," and it is true that no other guests are mentioned. The important relationship cemented by this meal seems to be between Nabal and his wine. Though his wife and servants are conspiring with his enemies, Nabal is feeling no pain: "Nabal's heart was good in him, and he was very drunk" (v. 36). Abigail consequently does not tell him "any small or great thing until the light of the morning. And when it was morning, when the wine left Nabal, then his wife told him these things . . . " (v. 37). She seems to wait until he will feel the full brunt of her message without the intervening cushion of the wine. Jobling concludes from this that Abigail is determined to hurt Nabal as deeply as possible. Robert Alter goes so far as to say that Abigail knows of an inherent weakness in her husband's heart and is trying to kill him with the timing and content of her message.[14] But it may simply be that Abigail waits until Nabal is sober because she wants him to remember what she tells him, or even to understand it.

We are not told that Nabal had a hangover, but it does seem a logical inference, given how drunk he is said to have been. So as David was, at least emotionally, in pain from lack of food and drink, now Nabal is in pain from an overabundance. He sits in the cold light of dawn, abandoned by his best friend, the wine, hearing what his wife has to say. What "things" does she tell him? Recall that very little has actually happened up to this point, and half of that Nabal himself was involved in. Abigail can only be informing him that she gave David and his men food and thus averted Nabal's own doom. We might expect Nabal to become angry at his wife and his servants and David, or conceivably to be relieved that he and his household are still alive. We have no reason to expect him to die inside, to lose his will to live.

But Nabal did not want to feed David or his men, arguing that his meat, bread, and drink were for his own shearers, his own men (v. 11). The banquet seems to argue that Nabal actually wanted the food for himself. As the wine leaves him, he hears that his food has left him, too; that the woman whose job is to nurture him has also left him to provide David with food. On the one hand, Nabal's heart dying within him makes sense as a reaction to Abigail's profound betrayal. She has taken Nabal's goods and offered them to another man; the sexual connotations here are no accident. The food becomes a metaphor for Abigail herself, the sexual property that belongs to Nabal but is already on its way to David. Abigail has in fact loaded herself onto a donkey after loading up the food and wine and sent herself after her gifts, as though she would be dessert.

The list of food that Abigail sends ahead of her invokes abundance, fertility, prosperity—all that is understood to emerge from a fruitful marriage, though as far as we know her actual marriage has borne no fruit in children. Similarly, Jacob, the pinnacle of the biblical focus on fertility, sends herds of livestock ahead of him, and brings his children and wives behind, when he meets his estranged brother, Esau. The message in both cases seems to be that there are benefits to a friendship with the gift-giver. An even greater resonance appears closer to our passage, in 2 Samuel 16:1–5. There, Ziba, the servant of Meribaal, meets the retreating David with "saddled asses laden with two hundred loaves of bread, an ephah of cakes of pressed raisins, an ephah of summer fruits, and a skin of wine" (2 Sam. 16: 1), an offering bearing a striking resemblance to Abigail's, minus the meat. Ziba offers all these to David and his young men because he also brings David the message that Meribaal has rebelled against David's kingship. Like Abigail, Ziba wants to make it clear that he is on David's side, despite the belligerent actions of his master.

But if through Abigail's culinary support David will eat and live, the same support means Nabal will die. When Nabal eats and drinks, thinking that he has left David and his men hungry, then "his heart is good in him" (v. 36). When he hears that David has been given food and drink, his heart dies. The two are mutually exclusive, as Nabal himself has implied in his rebuke of David. Abigail takes food from one to the other, which indirectly causes one to die while the other thrives. In a kind of simplified and subtler version of the equation of Mordecai and Haman, the woman's informal power, wielded through food and sexuality, becomes the means by which life and death are exchanged between the two men.

Though critics often point out the ways in which Nabal is a type for Saul, the story also draws out an equivalence between Nabal and David. Nabal, the fool, is twice described as a "son of Belial," often translated as "a wicked man" or "a son of wickedness." In the passage immediately following Ziba's offering of food to David, David also is referred to as a son of Belial by his most vocal enemy, Shimei. Shimei chooses to hurl this epithet at the moment when David is in full retreat, even ready to accept the stones and dust that Shimei throws along with his insults. As the King James translates, Shimei is shouting, "Come out, thou bloody man, thou son of Belial!" and accusing David of having reigned in Saul's stead, and of being punished now (with the rebellion of his son Absalom) for his bloody misdeeds. The very blood that

Abigail has diverted from David's hands has, in Shimei's judgment, landed there in any case, bringing the divine recompense Abigail saw herself as precluding. Nabal is a kind of
early prophecy of David's future self, at least from one angle.
At the moment that he meets Abigail, David is in between
rounds of restraining himself from killing Saul. But Saul will
die, and though his death is, like Nabal's, apparently at the
hands of God and for his own sins, the restraint David shows
so clearly here will become debatable by the time he
becomes the king, and nonexistent before he marries his next
wife.

LOVE AND FOOLISHNESS

Jobling assumes that Abigail is in love with David, and
laments that "perhaps the most chilling aspect of these stories
of women as pawns in royal power struggles is the way they
are processed as stories of women's love for men."[15] My question would be whether in this case that processing occurs in
the text or in the reading of it. Evidence of romantic desire
on Abigail's part is scant, at best. Initially, she is afraid of
David. The reader hears David instructing his men to "put
on, each man, his sword," and then hears Nabal's servant urge
Abigail to "think! And see what you can do, for disaster hangs
over our master and over the whole of his household" (v. 17).
Abigail's rush to placate, flatter, and befriend David is in
response to this impending disaster. She is not said, like Ruth,
Esther, or Judith, to bathe and perfume herself and put on her
best robes before going to meet David. Rather, she packs up
the food that she hopes will calm him and hurries out in
order to get to him before the killing begins. Somewhere in
her long speech, however, she seems to take on other ideas
besides saving her household. We hear for the first time that
she knows all about him; specifically, she knows that he will

be king. Whether she knew this about David before his arrival or has only just figured it out while talking to him, or whether it is an inspired piece of flattery that she has just invented, we can only guess, but she dwells on it at some length. Initially begging him only to forgive Nabal's offense, somewhere around verse 29 or 30 she seems to begin to hope that she may actually gain, rather than be completely destroyed, by this meeting. Certainly such a hope is expressed in her request that David remember her "when Yahweh brings good to my master" (v. 30).

Perhaps the fact that Abigail despises her husband leads readers to conclude that she loves David, though logically one does not necessarily follow the other. We might look at her request for David to remember her as emerging from her marriage to a bad man.[16] In that case, Abigail appears to hope that David might offer some way out, though whether she hopes to marry him or only to work for him like the servant she calls herself is not clear. Whichever hope she harbors, she nevertheless prevents David from killing Nabal. If she loves or even hopes in David and despises Nabal so much, why step between them? As Jobling points out, the danger of blood-guilt from which God and Abigail save David "seems to the reader to be suddenly plucked out of nowhere."[17] Jobling suspects that David's very bravado hints at the possibility that in fact Nabal would have emerged the victor from any confrontation, so that what Abigail actually saves him from is "a beating, or worse, at Nabal's hands."[18] But at this point in our story, David stands as the undefeated champion, running away from King Saul only because he is too loyal and scrupulous to commit regicide. In the whole of David's saga, in fact, he will only ever be defeated by himself, by the very staggering of heart that Abigail wishes away from him (v. 31). Nabal is a powerful man, but that only makes him a juicier target for David's strength, which after all is the strength of God.

The fact that Abigail wastes no time in answering David's summons to come and be his wife also does not indicate romantic love, but only that she recognizes that it would be better to be wife of the man who will be king than to remain the widow of a man whom she and God both despise. All things considered, marriage to David seems a pretty good option, if indeed she has any choice at all. More interesting is that David immediately thinks of marrying Abigail when he hears that Nabal is dead (v. 39b). Clearly the idea of taking her "as woman" has occurred to him before. Jobling does not conclude love from David's haste, but rather: "he surely experiences a desire that reciprocates Abigail's own."[19] David's desire for Abigail, then, only mirrors what appears in Jobling's reading to be the original article, that emerging from the woman.

Commentators often note the connections between this story and that of Bathsheba, who is also often read as the willful source of David's desire. In both stories David intends to kill a man and marry his wife. As in the comparison to Esther, Jael, and Judith, the comparison to Bathsheba leaves Abigail's story looking quite proper. In 1 Sam. 25, as opposed to 2 Sam. 11, there is no sexual relationship between the married woman and the king, until the woman becomes a widow and then David's wife. Similarly, and perhaps more importantly from the story's own point of view, the marriage in Abigail's case is not made possible by a murder, but by a death from natural and/or supernatural causes. In the end, this is a story of how, as Nathan explains to David after the latter's rape of Bathsheba, God was willing to give David whatever he wanted at no cost (2 Sam. 12:8). David gets the food, the wine, the land, the livestock, and the woman, without having to kill.

And Abigail—well, at least she is neither raped nor married to Nabal anymore, though as Jobling points out, entering David's harem is not exactly happily ever after. Ironically, the bloodguilt she postpones splatters onto David with the murder of Uriah the Hittite, and Abigail's own son, Amnon, becomes a part of the recompense that David must pay. Rape will happen, though Abigail prevents it at the moment. The very foolishness or wickedness, *nebalah,* that characterizes Nabal will crop up again in Amnon's treatment of Tamar, as Tamar begs him not to do this thing which is "an abomination"—*nebalah*—in Israel, trying in vain to convince him that he will thus be seen as a fool, *nebal* (2 Sam. 13:12–13). The two different uses of the word *nebal* and *nebalah* seem to have connotations of sexual immorality, in fact, and are used also of the rape of Dinah in Genesis 34. Abigail is up against rape in the persons of her current and her future husband, but manages to stave it off, if only for the moment. The reader is here alerted to the presence of rape and murder in David's story, a presence that connects this passage with David's rape of Bathsheba (2 Sam. 11) and Amnon's rape of Tamar (2 Sam. 13), and the murders occasioned by each. By then Abigail's character has dwindled to nothingness. Once Abigail prevents bloodguilt here, she is shut away with the other wives. The contemporary reader seeing her actions here can speculate the impossible: Had she remained public and in defiance of the rules of marriage, perhaps David's reign could have been as she predicted it, preserved from bloodguilt and divine recompense. But David, hearing her voice here, knows of nothing better to do with her than to "take her as woman"; i.e., to shut her up in the harem as one voiceless woman among the many. With her go David's better instincts and possibly his only advisor for peace.

While Abigail is married to a bad man, her goodness, beauty, and wisdom shine. She plays with the big boys in the stead of her worthless husband. Once David marries her, she disappears under his shadow, in more ways than one—giving birth to Amnon, a kind of shadow self of David—rebel, rapist, source of conflict, and generally a sore spot among the children of David's wives. If Abigail could see David's future and her own disappearance within it, then it is no wonder she tries to steer him down another path.

REFLECTION QUESTIONS

1. The author maintains that Abigail is not, or not necessarily, in love with David. Do you agree with this judgment? What significance does the question have for the interpretation of the story? How does it affect your understanding of who Abigail is?

2. To what extent does Abigail's story fit the pattern established by the other stories?

3. What is in the encounter with Abigail that changes David's mind? The food? Her words? Her gestures of obeisance?

4. How does the story affect our understanding of who David is at this point, or who he will be as king?

5. Do you know of contemporary examples of women who were admired initially by men for their spirit or unconventionality, but who seemed to lose those qualities in marriage?

— CONCLUSION —

JAEL, JUDITH, ESTHER, ABIGAIL ... HERODIAS

THOUGH THE FIVE STORIES discussed in these chapters could be arranged in other orders, leaving Abigail's "unmurder" of her husband for last seemed appropriate, as did the juxtaposition of Jael and Judith on the one hand, and Judith and Esther on the other. Having reached the stage of conclusions, though, what emerges from the foregoing are a series of issues and themes that are common to Jael, Judith, Esther, and Abigail (despite the fact that hers is not a murder), but not to the most recent text and the only one completely outside the Jewish canon, that of Herodias. Not the heroine nor even the main character of her own story, Herodias is the only one of these women judged unequivocally as evil by the text itself. While each of the others may act in unconventional and even shocking ways, what they do is ultimately right and good. What Herodias wants done and gets done, on the other hand, is in the eyes of the text, the death of "a righteous and holy man." Her breaking of gender rules is on this account presented as a great deal more wrong than that of the others—and her story is ultimately a great deal less possible to read as liberative for women in consequence.

MEN KILL, WOMEN FEED

Few activities are so universally assigned to one gender as is that of killing. As a rule, men are the warriors, the hunters, the sacrificers, and the professional butchers. Men kill. Our cultural instincts will supply us with reasons for this: Men were physically stronger; hunting required mobility that women with infants did not have; or, on the other hand, women cannot be trusted with killing power; they are too irrational, too easily persuaded. Feminists like myself may be tempted to conclude that this ancient assignment of roles reflects actually the greater connectedness of women to the cycles of life—rather than being excluded from the act of killing, women perhaps shunned it. Regardless of the rationales, most of which border on biological determinism, the rule that killers are men more or less stands to this day. But, as the biblical writers knew very well, rules are made to be broken. When women kill, it was and is news. It disturbs, unnerves, threatens a society that sees the rule itself as built on natural, eternal distinctions. The idea, the imagined scene of a woman killing a man becomes a way of lifting up both the traditional roles for men and women and the possibility of transgressing them.

If killing is understood to be the province of men, then maleness is in part at least defined by the power to kill. Women, conversely, are defined in the biblical text by their ability to give birth and to nurture. Yet the definition of nurturing as women's work is not as sharply defended as its male counterpart. Men from time to time are found cooking and feeding in the biblical text, without provoking shock or even remark. Jacob, for example cooks lentil stew to feed Esau and goat stew to feed his father.[1] Jesus in the gospel according to Mark is seen in the act of providing nourishment, even from or of his own body, to his followers. The rule, then, is not that only women can feed, but that women can only feed. They cannot kill. These stories about women who kill and feed seem to be about the clash, even about a perceived polarity, between these two activities. In these stories the interest in food seems to emerge from a concern with the woman's femaleness, her ability to feed and nurture, and how that comes into conflict—or fails to—with her ability to kill.

Yet, only three of these five women are actually providers of food. Jael, in a move that immediately evokes the mother, offers milk to Sisera. Esther prepares and hosts her banquets, which soften the king's heart toward her significantly. And Abigail loads her donkeys with massive gifts of food for David, which he does not eat. But Judith only attends the meal that Holofernes hosts, and Herodias does not even do that. For both of these who are not feeding the man, there is an emphasis on anti-commensality. When John the Baptist was a free man, he ate only locusts and wild honey—the reader cannot even imagine this imprisoned wild man sharing Herod's or Herodias's table. In her story, Judith only eats at all when it is a festival day or a sabbath, and yet makes a point of bringing her own food to Holofernes's table, and of its being fully sufficient for her needs. More interesting, even shocking, is the fact that these two who do not feed the man are the very two who serve the man as food. Both Judith and Herodias put their enemy's head where their food belongs— Judith having her maid stuff the head into her kosher food sack, while Herodias's daughter receives from Herod and gives to Herodias John the Baptist's head on a platter.

FOUR HEROIC WOMEN AND A MOTHER

Women in the Bible are most prominent as mothers. Even those who are not mothers often gain identity from their desire to be mothers (Jepthah's daughter mourns her virginity, for example, presumably for this reason), from their exclusion from being mothers (the raped Tamar's devastation is partly a result of her being thus excluded from proper marriage and childbirth), and in other ways from the existence of the role and goal of motherhood. So it is surely not coincidental that of the five biblical women examined here, though all have been or are married, only Herodias is a mother when we know her.

Jael's story is brief enough that any children she has had might have simply gone unmentioned. Yet the setting of her tent would be precisely where her children would be born and nurtured in their early years, so their complete absence here does suggest that they do not exist. Moreover, Jael's motherhood, though emphasized, is focused on Sisera. If Jael had an actual baby, the child would interrupt and intercept her treatment of Sisera as a baby; even the idea of an actual infant would seem to draw Jael's maternal qualities away from their task of sedating the man.

Judith likewise is childless, and in her case widowhood has freed her even from the complicating question of a husband's presence. She is on the one hand free to live as devoutly and to defend her people as fiercely as she wishes. On the other hand, we might conclude that the author found it impossible to marry her off, since she is so wise, so beautiful, and so frightening, that no man is either worthy of her or can stand up to her.

Esther's childlessness occurs despite her marriage to a living and present man. The narrator takes no note of it, which would seem strange were Esther not married to a Gentile. Her position of insider/outsider is both precarious and absolutely necessary on account of this marriage. She may not keep kosher, she may seduce and sleep with a gentile, but if Esther were in the business of bearing children to the gentiles, then she would have fallen from her position on the border and become something different altogether, more their victim than their queen.

In Abigail's case, the reader who asks the question of children can only be grateful that Nabal did not manage to reproduce, so far as we know. As in Esther's case, the woman's unremarked childlessness may spare us a more vivid sense of her consummated sexual relationship with a fool. Though she comes to David a well-to-do widow, Abigail has unalloyed disgust for her first husband. The absence of children, and Nabal's inability to even communicate with her, thus leave the reader with a sense that Abigail has been saving her best self for David.

Herodias is once again the exception that makes the rule, since her mother-child connection is precisely what allows her to kill, and her killing is not in any way justified. She is an "unnatural" mother and an illicit one, since either the girl is hers by her first husband, whose rights to her womb she has failed to protect, or by her second, who has no rights to her womb at all. Her daughter appears unusually connected to and dependent on Herodias, turning to her even to ask, in effect, "What do I want?" and then owning Herodias's desire as her own with seeming enthusiasm. While the others are not mothers at all, or not until later stories in Abigail's case, Herodias is a mother with a vengeance, in every sense.

Yet Herodias, like Judith, does not feed. Herodias is not even present at the banquet, which is for Herod's birthday and features Herod as host to entirely male guests. If Herodias feeds anyone, it may perhaps be her own daughter, as it is through Herodias's hatred that the girl receives from Herod something framed as food. The fact that Herodias has a daughter, whom she is in this sense determined to feed, renders her motherhood evil in the story's eyes. Her nourishment is not for men—it rather consists of a man—so from the male perspective of the story, there is no sense in which it can be called good. Herodias has her own interests at heart, not those of her people. This is represented, embodied, in her daughter, who constitutes a loyalty, an alliance that has nothing to do with men and can be used against them. A woman with a child has reasons of her own to act; if such a woman kills, she likely does not do so in the interests of men. Among other possibilities, Herodias may represent, in fact, the dangerous, overly potent connections inherent in motherhood itself.

Perhaps precisely to avoid this kind of judgment, the other four women are presented as childless when the killing takes place. If they feed, they feed men; if they mother, they mother in this sense, offering pleasure, intimacy, and nourishment to a warrior or king. On the one hand, each woman's desire and power to kill would seem more wrong alongside a power to give life. On the other hand, a woman cannot, it seems, both mother a man in order to kill him and mother a child in order to promote its life. The pleasures of being nurtured, being mothered, and the power of mothering cannot be seen in both their dangerous and their vital aspects at the same time.

WITHIN EVERY GREAT WOMAN . . .

When a woman kills a man, and even more so a man who is himself a killer, a warrior or king whose power to kill defines him, the act is in itself a crossing of clearly marked boundaries, as the woman moves into the killing fields that are the territory of men. In each story, then, the issue of boundaries comes into play, and in each the woman (or girl in the case of Herodias and her daughter) manages by markedly feminine means to cross the boundaries established by men, to get to a man, most often the man she wants to see dead. Though the boundary at the basis of all of these may be that between male and female, there is something about the woman's femaleness that not only makes her own boundaries permeable, as we might expect, but allows her to penetrate the boundaries of the men. It is as if the rules, having been made by and for men, do not entirely apply to women.

At the same time, and along the same lines, rise the issues of us and them that are so prominent in all of these stories. In each story there are two opposing camps or peoples, and the woman caught in between the two. Much of the deception that plays out in the food and the sexuality consists of the woman's pretending to be with one group, to the extent that even the reader begins to wonder whether she is or not, until finally we discover her true loyalties in the murder. The female nurturing and feeding, then, is for the purposes of deception and manipulation; the male killing is the true identity of the woman revealed. In her truest identity, then, she is male.

The exception to this working out of tensions between the good guys and bad guys is the story of Herodias, in which the tension is resolved beforehand—we know at once that Herod has killed John, so that John's tiny place in the story of his own execution becomes a very small place for the reader's sympathies to stand. The tension navigated by the girl in this story is not between good and bad, but between conflicting and finally cooperating aspects of the ruling evil.

A threat of rape is in the air in all but Herodias's story, though it seems not to be a genuine threat in Esther's. In the Bible, rape constitutes a possible, an almost but not-quite-acceptable justification for killing—see for example the vengeance killings of Shechem in Genesis and of Amnon in 2 Samuel, both of which are neither approved of nor punished by the victim's father. It makes sense then that there is no threat of rape from the doomed John the Baptist, and Herodias's murderous intent is left unjustified. Interestingly, in the case of the other four women, the hints at rape remain hints, or in Esther's case a false accusation; rape never explicitly happens to these women involved in murder. Indeed, the hints of rape must remain such, since a rape victim in the biblical text is by definition passive, devastated, finished—no more likely to avenge her own pain than is a murder victim. Jael, Judith, Esther, and Abigail are in this sense the opposite of the biblical portrait of rape victims. These are women actively intervening to maintain their own and the nation's sovereignty. Staving off invasion and entry, Judith-as-national-metaphor cannot then marry any mortal man, but must maintain her own boundaries as surely as she has penetrated the enemy's.[2] The other three women are less idealized and exceptional, and less notably chaste, but remain somewhat metaphorical, emblems of a national integrity to the extent that, when in danger of being raped, penetrated, invaded, they make sure the would-be rapist dies instead.

WORKS CITED

Alter, Robert. *The David Story: A Translation with Commentary of 1 and 2 Samuel.* New York: W. W. Norton and Company, 1999.

Assis, Elie. "The Choice to Serve God and Assist His People." *Biblica* 85 (2004): 82–90.

Bach, Alice. "Calling the Shots: Directing Salome's Dance of Death." *Semeia* 74 (1996): 103–26.

———. *Women, Seduction, and Betrayal in Biblical Narrative.* Cambridge, Eng.: Cambridge University Press, 1997.

Bal, Mieke. *Death and Dissymmetry: The Politics of Coherence in Judges.* Chicago: University of Chicago Press, 1988.

———. *Murder and Difference: Gender, Genre, and Scholarship on Sisera's Death.* Bloomington: Indiana University Press, 1988.

Bauer, Walter. *A Greek-English lexicon of the New Testament and other early Christian literature.* Trans. and ed., William F. Arndt and F. Wilbur Gingrich. 2d ed. Chicago: University of Chicago Press, 1979.

Beal, Timothy K. *Esther.* Berit Olam. Collegeville, Minn.: Liturgical Press, 1999.

Boyle, Marjorie O'Rourke. "The Law of the Heart: The Death of a Fool (1 Samuel 25)." *Journal of Biblical Literature* 120, no. 3 (2001): 401–27.

Craven, Toni. "The Book of Judith in the Context of the Twentieth Century Studies of the Apocryphal/Deuterocanonical Books." *Currents in Biblical Research* 1, no. 3 (April 2003): 190.

Delorme, Jean. "John the Baptist's Head—the Word Perverted: A Reading of a Narrative (Mark 6:14–29)." *Semeia* 81 (1998): 115–29.

Doob Sakenfeld, Katherine. "Deborah, Jael, and Sisera's Mother: Reading the Scripture in Cross-Cultural Context." In *Women, Gender, and Christian Community*, edited by Jane Dempsey Douglass and James F. Kay, 13–22. Louisville, Ky.: Westminster/John Knox Press, 1997.

Dorothy, Charles. *The Books of Esther: Structure, Genre, and Textual Integrity.* JSOTSS 187 (Journal for the Study of Old Testament Supplement Series). Sheffield, Eng.: Sheffield Academic Press, 1997.

Douglas, Mary. *Purity and Danger: An Analysis of the Concepts of Pollution and Taboo.* New York: Praeger, 1966.

Duran, Nicole Wilkinson. "Return of the Disembodied or How John the Baptist Lost His Head." In *Reading Communities Reading Texts: Essays in Honor of Daniel Patte*, edited by Gary A. Phillips and Nicole Wilkinson Duran, 277–91. Harrisburg, Pa.: Trinity International Press, 2002.

Fewell, Danna Nolan and David M. Gunn. "Controlling Perspectives: Women, Men, and the Authority of Violence in Judges 4 and 5." *Journal of the American Academy of Religion* 58, no. 3. (Autumn 1990): 389–411.

———. *Gender, Power, and Promise: The Subject of the Bible's First Story.* Nashville: Abingdon Press, 1993.

Focant, Camille. "La tête du prophete sur un plat ou, l'anti-repas d'alliance (Mc 6.14–29)." *New Testament Studies* 47(2001)/3:334–53.

Fox, Michael V. *Character and Ideology in Esther.* Grand Rapids, Mich.: Eerdmans Publishing, 1991.

Girard, Rene. "Scandal and the Dance: Salome in the Gospel of Mark." *New Literary History* 15, no. 2 (1984): 311–24.

Green, Barbara. "Enacting Imaginatively the Unthinkable: 1 Samuel 25 and the Story of Saul." *Biblical Interpretation* 11, no. 1:1–23.

Gunn, David M. "Biblical Women and Subjectivity: From Abelard to Harriet Beecher Stowe." *SBL Forum* 6/1/05–7/5/05.

Harvey, Charles D. *Finding Morality in the Diaspora? Moral Ambiguity and Transformed Morality in the Books of Esther.* New York: Walter de Gruyter, 2003

Jay, Nancy. *Throughout Your Generations Forever.* Chicago: University of Chicago Press, 1992.

Jobling, David. *1 Samuel.* Berit Olam. Collegeville, Minn.: Liturgical Press, 1998.

Kelber, Werber. *Oral and Written Gospel: The Hermeneutics of Speaking and Writing in the Synoptic Tradition, Mark, and Paul.* Philadelphia: Fortress Press, 1983.

Klein, Lillian R. "Honor and Shame in Esther." In *A Feminist Companion Esther, Judith, and Susanna,* edited by Athalya Brenner, 149–75. Sheffield, Eng.: Sheffield Academic Press, 1995.

Levenson, Jon D. *Death and Resurrection of the Beloved Son.* New Haven, Conn.: Yale University Press, 1993.

———. *Esther. The Old Testament Library.* Louisville, Ky.: Westminster/John Knox, 1997.

———. "1 Samuel 25 as Literature and as History." *Catholic Biblical Quarterly* 40 (1978): 11–28.

Levine, Amy-Jill. "Sacrifice and Salvation: Otherness and Domestication in the Book of Judith." In *No One Spoke Ill of Her,* edited by James C. Vanderkam, 17–30. Atlanta: Scholars Press, 1992.

Matthews, Victor, and Donald Benjamin. "Jael: Host or Judge?" *Bible Today* 30 (1992): 292–94.

Merchant, Peter. "Inhabiting the Interspace: De Tabley, Judges, Jael." *West Virginia University Bulletin* 36/2: 187–203.

Moore, Carey A. *Judith*. Vol. 40, *The Anchor Bible*. New York: Doubleday and Co., 1985.

Niditch, Susan. "Eroticism and Death in the Tale of Jael." In *Gender and Difference in Ancient Israel,* edited by Peggy L. Day. Minneapolis, Minn.: Fortress Press, 1989.

Otzen, Benedikt. *Tobit and Judith.* London, Eng.: Sheffield Academic Press, 2002.

Schneider, Tammi. *Judges.* Berit Olam no. 4. Collegeville, Minn.: Liturgical Press, 2000.

Stocker, Margarita. *Judith, Sexual Warrior: Women and Power in Western Culture.* New Haven, Conn.: Yale University Press, 1998.

van Dijk-Hemmes, Fokkelien. "Mothers and a Mediator in the Song of Deborah." In *A Feminist Companion to Judges,* edited by Athalya Brenner, 110–14. Sheffield, Eng.: Sheffield University Press, 1993.

Van Wolde, Ellen. "Deborah and Ya'el in Judges 4–5." In *On Reading Prophetic Texts: Gender-Specific and Related Studies in Memory of Fokkelien van Dijk-Hemmes,* edited by Bob Becking and Meindert Dijkstra, 283–95. Biblical Interpretation Series. Leiden Netherlands: E. J. Brill, 1996.

White, Sidnie Ann. "In the Steps of Deborah and Jael: Judith as Heroine." In *No One Spoke Ill of Her: Essays on Judith,* edited by James C. VanderKam, 5–16. Atlanta: Scholars Press, 1992.

Wills, Lawrence. *Jew in the Court of the Foreign King.* Harvard Dissertation Series, no. 26. Minneapolis, Minn.: Fortress Press, 1990.

Wyler, Bea. "Esther: The Incomplete Emancipation of a Queen." In *A Feminist Companion to Esther, Judith, and Susanna,* edited by Athalya Brenner, 111–35. Sheffield, Eng.: Sheffield Academic Press, 1995.

NOTES

INTRODUCTION
FOOD, DRINK, SEX, AND DEATH
The Symbolism of Eating and Drinking

1. For a uniquely insightful treatment revealing sacrificial logic in biblical texts, see Jon D. Levenson, *Death and Resurrection of the Beloved Son* (New Haven: Yale University Press, 1993).

2. Compare Jesus' prediction in the synoptics that he will be betrayed by "one who is eating with me . . . one who is dipping bread into the bowl with me" (Mark 14:18, 20). The bitterness of the betrayal is outlined by the fact that betrayer and betrayed have shared food.

3. I will continue to talk about the stories as focusing on murder, although in Abigail's case, the term is a stretch. In the chapter exploring her story, the association of Nabal's natural, fortunate death with the other murders will become clearer.

4. Alice Bach, *Women, Seduction, and Betrayal in Biblical Narrative* (Cambridge: Cambridge University Press, 1997), 184.

CHAPTER 1. JAEL: *Milk and Murder,*

The Brief and Brutal Story

1. See David M. Gunn, "Biblical Women and Subjectivity: From Abelard to Harriet Beecher Stowe," *SBL Forum* 6/1/05–7/5/05 for a review of some treatments of the story over the centuries.

2. Katherine Doob Sakenfeld, "Deborah, Jael, and Sisera's Mother: Reading the Scripture in Cross-Cultural Context," in *Women, Gender, and Christian Community,* ed. E. Jane Dempsey Douglass and James F. Kay (Louisville, Ky.: Westminster/John Knox Press, 1997), 13. See also Tammi Schneider's remark that modern scholars do not like the verses that exult in Sisera's murder in Judges 5, and "express their displeasure by not commenting on them" in *Judges,* Berit Olam no. 4, 92. (Collegeville, MN: Liturgical Press, 2000), 92.

3. Mieke Bal, *Murder and Difference: Gender, Genre, and Scholarship on Sisera's Death* (Bloomington, IN: Indiana University Press, 1988); Danna Nolan Fewell and David M. Gunn, "Controlling Perspectives: Women, Men, and the Authority of Violence in Judges 4 and 5," *Journal of the American*

Academy of Religion 58, no. 3 (Autumn 1990): 389–90.

4. Werner Kelber, *Oral and Written Gospel: The Hermeneutics of Speaking and Writing in the Synoptic Tradition, Mark, and Paul* (Philadelphia: Fortress Press, 1983), 15.

5. Sidnie Ann White, "In the Steps of Deborah and Jael: Judith as Heroine," in *No One Spoke Ill of Her: Essays on Judith,* ed. James C. VanderKam (Atlanta: Scholars Press, 1992), 9. More on Judith as a rewritten Jael in the next chapter.

6. Ibid., 8.

7. Mieke Bal, *Death and Dyssemetry: The Politics of Coherence in Judges* (Chicago: University of Chicago Press, 1988), 212.

8. Ellen Van Wolde, "Deborah and Ya'el in Judges 4–5," in *On Reading Prophetic Texts: Gender-Specific and Related Studies in Memory of Fokkelien van Dijk-Hemmes.* ed. Bob Becking and Meindert Dijkstra, Biblical Interpretation Series (Leiden: E. J. Brill, 1996), 292.

9. Ibid., 295.

10. See Peter Merchant, who asserts that the story disturbed Victorian readers "not least because in stressing the neutrality of Jael and her husband . . . the text left her with no adequate motive for murdering her guest in his sleep" ("Inhabiting the Interspace: De Tabley, Judges, 'Jael'" [West Virginia University bulletin 36/2: 187]). De Tabley's poem supplies Jael with the motive of her own glory.

11. Fewell and Gunn, 395.

12. Sakenfeld, "Deborah, Jael, and Sisera's Mother," 20–21.

13. Victor Matthews and Donald Benjamin, "Jael: Host or Judge?" *Bible Today* 30 (1992): 292–94.

14. Ibid., 295.

15. Ibid., 294.

16. Mieke Bal holds that to read Sisera as intending rape has the added effect of dimissing the possibility that Jael's action is a political one, emerging from her own desire to join the battle (*Death and Dyssymmetry: The Politics of Coherence in Judges* [Chicago: University of Chicago Press, 1988], 212).

17. Elie Assis, "The Choice to Serve God and Assist His People," *Biblica* 85 (2004): 82–90.

18. See Bal, *Death and Dyssymetry,* 213–14; Matthews and Benjamin, 295, for example.

19. Fewell and Gunn, "Controlling Perspectives," 393, where they further note that the same Hebrew word *patah* is used regarding the opening or entrance of the tent in verse 20.

20. White, "In the Steps of Deborah and Jael," 9.

21. Fewell and Gunn, "Controlling Prespectives," 393.

22. On the sexual connotations of the sibilance and scene's interpretation as sexual in rabbinic literature, see Assis, "The Choice to Serve God," 84.

23. Ibid., 83.

24. Bal, *Murder and Difference,* 130.

25. Fokkelien van Dijk-Hemmes remarks, "she bears him for death, not for life," in "Mothers and a Mediator in the Song of Deborah," *A Feminist Companion to Judges,* ed. Athalya Brenner (Sheffield: Sheffield University Press, 1993), 112.

26. For connotations of the Hebrew word *lat,* see Susan Niditch, "Eroticism and Death in the Tale of Jael," in *Gender and Difference in Ancient Israel,* ed. Peggy L. Day (Minneapolis: Fortress Press), 45b, 1989.

27. On the emphasis on women as mothers in biblical narrative, see Fewell and Gunn, *Gender, Power and Promise* (Nashville: Abirgdon Press,

1993), 68.

28. Merchant, "Inhabiting the Interspace," 189.

29. Tammi Schneider, "Judges," Berit Olam no. 4 (Collegeville, Minn.: Liturgical Press, 2000), 80.

30. Bal, *Death and Dyssymetry*, 215.

31. Fewell and Gunn, "Controlling Perspectives," 303; see also Van Wolde, "Deborah and Ya'el in Judges 4–5," 293, who suggests that the word be translated "throat."

32. Schneider suggests that this is not the scribe's or writer's error, but the character's (80).

33. Quoted in Gunn, "Biblical Women and Subjectivity."

34. Fewell and Gunn, "Controlling Perspectives," 401.

35. Fewell and Gunn, *Gender, Power, and Promise*, 89.

CHAPTER 2. JUDITH: *A Chaste and Kosher Killing*

1. Nancy Jay argued convincingly for matrilineal strains in the patriarchal narratives in *Throughout Your Generations Forever* (Chicago: University of Chicago Press, 1992), 97ff.

2. Cf. Amy-Jill Levine, who holds that Judith outshines her insignificant (other than Israel) ancestors, and provides Simeon with otherwise nonexistent descendants (Gen. 39:7; "Amy-Jill Levine, "Sacrifice and Salvation," in *No One Spoke Ill of Her*, ed. James C. Vanderkam ([Atlanta: Scholars Press, 1992], 21).

3. Walter Bauer, *A Greek-English Lexicon of the New Testament and other early Christian Literature*. Trans. and ed. William F. Arndt and F. Wilbur Gingrich, 2d ed. (Chicago: University of Chicago Press, 1979), *"allogeneis,"* 39.

4. Levine, "Sacrifice and Salvation," 22.

5. Ibid., 19.

6. Mary Douglas, *Purity and Danger: An Analysis of the Concepts of Pollution and Taboo* (New York: Praeger, 1966).

7. Levine, "Sacrifice and Salvation," 22.

8. Margarita Stocker, *Judith, Sexual Warrior: Women and Power in Western Culture* (New Haven: Yale University Press, 1998), 6.

9. Levine, "Sacrifice and Salvation," 24.

10. Stocker, *Judith, Sexual Warrior*, 7.

11. Levine, "Sacrifice and Salvation," 22.

12. Stocker, *Judith, Sexual Warrior*, 7.

13. Ibid., 10.

14. Benedikt Otzen, *Tobit and Judith* (London: Sheffield Academic Press, 2002).

15. Stocker, *Judith, Sexual Warrior*, 8; Levine, "Sacrifice and Salvation," 21.

16. Toni Craven, "The Book of Judith in the Context of the Twentieth Century Studies of the Apocryphal/ Deuterocanonical Books," in *Currents in Biblical Research* 13, no. 3 (April 2003): 190, citing Torrey.

17. Levine, "Sacrifice and Salvation," 18.

18. Stocker, *Judith, Sexual Warrior*, 15.

CHAPTER 3. ESTHER: *Sleeping (and Drinking) with the Enemy*

1. Bea Wyler, "Esther: The Incomplete Emancipation of a Queen," in *A Feminist Companion to Esther, Judith, and Susanna*, ed. Athalya Brenner (Sheffield: Sheffield Academic Press, 1995), 113, 115.

2. Jon D. Levenson, *Esther, The Old Testament Library* (Louisville: Westminster/John Knox, 1997), 14.

3. The complex textual issues surrounding the story can be read as testifying likewise to its brand of native

foreignness. Significantly varying versions of Esther include the Masoretic, the Septuagint, and two other Greek translations. Each Greek version differs from the Hebrew in reinserting God, theology, and religious practice into what is in the Hebrew a remarkably secular text. Yet Timothy Beal and others believe that these religious and theological concerns are not simply absent in the MT, but have been erased from a still-earlier, now-nonexistent Hebrew version. The issue then becomes whether to take Esther as authoritative in its Hebrew or Greek version—whether, in fact, this fundamentally diaspora text may be better read in a second, diaspora language, than in its native Hebrew. I will be reading the Masoretic since it remains the earliest of the extant versions.

4. Among the memorable moments of this hilarious sketch was Murphy as Mr. White, in whiteface, discovering that when no blacks are present, white bank officers give loans to other whites freely: "Pay us back anytime," the bank official tells him, "or don't. We don't care." http://snltranscripts. jt.org/84/84iwhitelikeeddie.phtml

5. Levenson, *Esther,* 48.

6. Ibid.

7. Timothy K. Beal, *Esther,* Berit Olam (Collegeville: Liturgical Press, 1999), 2.

8. Michael V. Fox, *Character and Ideology in Esther* (Grand Rapids, Mich.: Eerdmans Publishing, 1991), 158.

9. Lillian R. Klein, "Honor and Shame in Esther," in *A Feminist Companion Esther, Judith, and Susanna,* Ed. Athalya Brenner. (Sheffield: Sheffield Academic Press, 1995), 154.

10. Klein, "Honor and Shame," 154.

11. Fox, *Character and Ideology,* 173.

12. *The Books of Esther: Structure, Genre, and Textual Integrity,* JSOTSS 187 (Sheffield: Sheffield Academic Press, 1997), 306.

13. Charles D. Harvey, *Finding Morality in the Diaspora?* (New York: Walter de Gruyter, 2003), 28.

CHAPTER 4. HERODIAS: *Banquet and Seduction in the Realm of Wrong*

1. Most interpreters assume that Herod is wrong about this, and that the reader knows better, since we saw John the Baptist baptizing Jesus back in Chapter 1. I am not so sure. The idea seems to be not that Jesus is John reincarnated (which would necessitate Jesus having been born after John died, and is in any case not a particularly Mediterranean concept), but that Jesus' power is fueled by the murdered spirit of John. Since the timing of John's death is unclear, it does not seem impossible that the gospel sees John's spirit as at least one contributing factor.

2. Camille Focant, "La tête du prophete sur un plat ou, l'antirepas d'alliance (Mc 6.14–29)" in *New Testament Studies* 47, no. 3 (2001): 341.

3. Cf. Focant (341), who wonders how long John has been in prison, when exactly he was executed, and how long Herodias has been waiting for her opportunity.

4. This is as opposed to the reading of Rene Girard, who claims without much evidence that "the emphasis is not on legality here" ("Scandal and the Dance: Salome in the Gospel of Mark," *New Literary History,* 15, no. 2 [1984]: 312). The verb *exesti* is consistently translated "it is lawful," and elsewhere in Mark clearly refers to matters of law—Mk. 2:24, 26; 3:4. See

also Mt. 12:2, 4, 10, 12, and 1 Cor.
6:12; 10:23.

5. Josephus also records a story of
Agrippa petitioning Caligula not to
put up a statue of himself in the temple. Pleased with the lavish dinner
Agrippa provides, the emperor offers
to grant any request: "Everything that
may contribute to thy happiness shall
be at thy service, and that cheerfully,
and so far as my ability will reach."
Like Esther, Agrippa defers making his
request once, saying he has served the
emperor in hopes of gain, then when
Caligula presses him, Agrippa asks that
the statue not be erected (*Antiquities*,
XVIII, viii, 7). Caligula dies shortly
thereafter, making the whole point
moot.

6. Lawrence M. Wills, *Jew in the
Court of the Foreign King* Harvard
Dissertation Series, no. 26
(Minneapolis: Fortress Press, 1990), 10.

7. Nicole Wilkinson Duran,
"Return of the Disembodied or How
John the Baptist Lost His Head," in
*Reading Communities Reading Texts:
Essays in Honor of Daniel Patte,* ed.
Gary A. Phillips and Nicole Wilkinson
Duran. (Harrisburg, Pa.: Trinity
International Press, 2002), 281–83.

8. Jean Delorme, "John the Baptist's
Head—the Word Perverted: A
Reading of a Narrative (Mark
6:14–29)," *Semeia* 81(1998): 123.

9. The daughter is never called
"Salome" in this story or in Matthew's
version. The name Salome appears in
Mark 16:1, as one of the women at
the tomb. The first century Jewish his-
torian Josephus says that the name of
Herodias's daughter was Salome
(*Antiquities* XVIII 5:4), but does not
cite her as instrumental in John the
Baptist's execution.

10. Alice Bach, "Calling the Shots:

Directing Salome's Dance of Death,"
Semeia 74 (1996): 107.

11. Some manuscripts read "his
daughter, Herodias," while others read
"the daughter of Herodias herself."
Each is awkward in its own way. Most
translations go with the second, as
does the Gospel of Matthew, in part
because within the story the girl acts
more like her mother's daughter.

12. According to the Georgia
Center for Children, "Stepfathers are 7
times more likely to [sexually] abuse
than biological fathers; however, abuse
by a biological parent tends to be
more severe. (A child who is abused
by a biological parent is at higher risk
of sustaining an injury from the abuse
than those abused by a non-biological
parent.)" http://www.georgiacenter-
forchildren.org/statistics.html

13. Bach, "Calling the Shots," 112.

14. Ibid., 108.

15. Girard, "Scandal and the Dance,"
318.

16. Delorme, "John the Baptist's
Head," 124.

17. Ibid, 122.

CHAPTER 5. ABIGAIL: *Murder,
Shalom, and the Lack Thereof*

1. David Jobling, *1 Samuel,* Berit
Olam (Collegeville, Minn.: Liturgical
Press, 1998), 156.

2. Ibid., 158.

3. Barbara Green, "Enacting
Imaginatively the Unthinkable: 1
Samuel 25 and the Story of Saul,"
Biblical Interpretation 11, no.1: 11.

4. Green, "Enacting
Imaginatively," 7.

5. Jon D. Levenson, "1 Samuel 25
as Literature and as History," *Catholic
Biblical Quarterly* 40 (1978): 15.

6. Marjorie O'Rourke Boyle, "The
Law of the Heart: The Death of a Fool

(1 Samuel 25)," *Journal of Biblical Literature* 120, no. 3 (2001): 415.

7. Levenson, "I Samuel 25," 15.

8. Green, "Enacting Imaginatively," 13.

9. I am indebted for this questionable insight to my seminary roommates Catherine Candlish and Linda Even, with whom I shared long conversations about which male animals actually could urinate against a wall.

10. If I were more of a historical critic, I would guess that Abigail's speech has been pieced together or edited in some way, and its disjointed quality results from that process. But my focus is on the text as it stands, in which Abigail appears to some degree to be babbling.

11. Boyle, "Law of the Heart," 423.

12. Ibid., 418.

13. Ibid., 419.

14. Robert Alter, *The David Story* (New York: W.W. Norton and Company, 1999), 112.

15. Jobling, *1 Samuel,* 160.

16. Jobling adds, "if we accept her side of the story" (158). But the idea that Nabal is like his name is first introduced by the narrator, not by Abigail, and it is confirmed by his servant, by David, and by everything Nabal says and does.

17. Jobling, *1 Samuel,* 157.

18. Ibid., 156.

19. Ibid., 156, 158.

CONCLUSION

1. Jacob is in fact quite involved with the provision of food. These two examples are the ways in which he deceives and gets the better of his brother Esau, in both cases by way of feeding. He then reconciles with Esau by parading a great deal of potential food in front of him (followed by his children and wives), and then sharing a meal with him. It may not be coincidental, given the centrality of feeding to Jacob's story, that he was his mother's favorite son, and that she mentors him in feeding/deceiving at one point. Notably as well, Jacob, despite his many conflicts, is not a killer.

2. Levine suggests that the only husband good enough for Judith is Yahweh (Sacrifice and Saluation," 22).